FRESHLY REMEMBER'D

A fresh look at the career of Wally Berger of the Boston
Braves, one of the greatest outfielders in the National League
during the Depression Decade (1930-1940), and one of the most
neglected by the Baseball Writers of America.

By:

Walter Anton Berger and

George Morris Snyder

Artist:

Jack Spencer McClain

Cover Design

and Illustrations

But he'll remember with advantages

What feats he did that day. Then shall our names,

Familiar in his mouth as household words ...

Be in their flowing cups freshly remember'd.

SHAKESPEARE

King Henry V, Act IV, Scene 3.

He was a competitor of the first rank,
and he won the ultimate prize: HONOR

. . . *freshly remember'd*

SCHNEIDER/McGUIRK PRESS

BY
WALTER ANTON BERGER
AND
GEORGE MORRIS SNYDER

This book is dedicated to

MARTHA BERGER
HARRIET NEMICCOLO
DIANE AND RON WALL
KENT AND RHEA SNYDER

And to the memory of

WALTER ANTON BERGER (1905-1988)
ANITA LINCE SNYDER, Ph. D. (1944-1992)

International Standard Book Number **0-9639330-0-0.**

Published by George Snyder.

Additional copies may be ordered from:

George M. Snyder
SCHNEIDER/MCGUIRK Press
Post Office Box 1404
Redondo Beach, CA 90278

$20.00

CONTENTS

ACKNOWLEDGMENTS

Martha Berger, devoted wife for over a half-century, always available and helpful. The perfect match for Wally.

Ron Wall, in whose barber shop it all began and continued, and his wife, Diane, for unbounded spirit and support, and a great All-Star Game party.

Ralph Livingstone, who introduced me to Wally, and for some inexplicable reason migrated to Modesto.

June McClain, wife of the artist. A constant supplier of aid and comfort beyond measure.

Dick Beverage, author and researcher. Helpful consultant and longtime friend of Wally.

The late *Foster Dean*, former Mayor of Manhattan and elder statesman. He made his spacious office available for the Zip Dumovich interview.

Zip Dumovich played with Wally at Pocatello in 1927 and against him in the PCL. A short stay with the Chicago Cubs. Good interview by Zip.

Vernon Mason, father of Dr. Robert Mason, who knew Wally at the Kettle. "Small World Department:" He attended Mission High with Wally and teammate Joe Cronin in 1922. He sent a team picture and remembrances from Yountville, California.

Sol Rogers, member of the Knot-Hole Gang in the Thirties in Boston. Saw Wally play many times. For his campaign for Wally to the Hall of Fame.

All the staff and regulars at the Kettle Restaurant, with *Iola Lordanich* at the helm, who for a decade made our mornings at breakfast so pleasant.

The informal Kettle Breakfast Committee to Promote the Consideration of Wally Berger to the National Baseball Hall of Fame:

Willie Atkinson	Heidi Crawford	Dr. Bob Mason
Dwight Andrews	William Fee	Michael Newfield
Burnett Bourgeois	Mike Gerber	Dr. David Ronfeldt
Bob Brigham	Richard Gonzales	Walter Slike
Dr. Anita Green	Gwen Van Orsdel	
	Denise Coca *(Chairperson)*	

The Sports Department of the Boston *Globe* for printing our letter of 1981, which got such a surprising response from fans of the Thirties, and for Paul Harber's obituary for Wally in 1988, with his excellent summary of Wally's career.

The Braves' Fans of the Thirties from all over Massachusetts and beyond who responded so generously to Wally's letter in the *Globe*. Their names are listed in the section titled "The Paying Critics."

The Manhattan Beach Public Library for securing for us the microfilms of the sports pages of the Los Angeles *Times* (1930-39).

The Publisher and staff of the *Beach Reporter* (Manhattan Beach) for their coverage of the hometown hero, especially on his return to Chicago for the 50th Anniversary of the All-Star Game in 1983, and *Mike Hamer's* extensive interview with pictures in the edition for February 25, 1988.

Daniel Cerone, writer and director, for his brilliant video interview about Wally and the Hall of Fame.

Jeff Floto, Editor of *The Diamond Angle* (Kaunakakai, Hawaii), and Associate Editor Bob Brigham (Manhattan Beach) for counsel and encouragement.

Syndicated columnist for the Los Angeles *Times* and Pulitzer Prize recipient *Jim Murray*, for his afternoon visit and interview. It was to be Wally's last interview (1988), most appropriately conducted by a sports writer of the first rank.

Joe Strapac of Shade Tree Books for his professional guidance in our venture in self-publishing.

Joe Ferrell, long-time colleague and specialist in graphic arts, for helpful suggestions and advice.

AND to the many kind people over the years who have expressed interest, good wishes and a promise to buy the book, thank you very much.

AND to the BEER DRINKERS' HALL OF FAME, a little bar somewhere between Pasadena and Monrovia, for putting things in perspective.

FOREWORD

Ralph Livingstone slipped the protective cover off my shoulders and indicated with a flourish that he had finished cuttting my hair. As I got up, he turned to a large man who sat in a waiting chair talking with Ron Wall, and said to me, "George, this is Wally Berger – he was a big star with the Boston Braves back in the Thirties."

Wally stood up. In his 73rd year he stood as straight, tall and dignified as he had been when he performed for Boston fans in 1930. We shook hands and exchanged greetings. Then I paid Ralph for my haircut, and with the usual pleasantries, left the barber shop.

It was the most fitting place to meet an old-time ball player. When Wally was playing in the Twenties and Thirties, the town barber shop, along with the general store, the pool hall, the garage, the gas station and the drug store formed the third league – the "hot stove league," the largest league of all. Millions of fans in town and country gathered there to replay the games, argue about players and teams and wager on almost anything related to baseball. Ron has a picture of his father's barber shop on the wall. It is a nostalgic reminder of those times.

Later that week I bumped into Wally at the Kettle Restaurant, where we discovered we were both regulars for breakfast. We shared the friendly presence of other regulars and were served by charming and percipient women. Often we sat next to each other at the counter and talked.

During my next visit to the library, I looked up Walter Anton Berger in the Encyclopedia of Baseball (Macmillan) and in other references. (As a high school student, of course, I had read about him in the sports pages of the Philadelphia papers, but my home-run heroes of the time were Jimmy Foxx, Al Simmons and Chuck Klein.) Not only did I find out what a great player Wally had been, but also discovered that his major-league career spanned the "depression decade."

In later conversations I became aware of how diligently and persistently he had prepared for that career during the entire decade which preceded it, beginning in 1920 with the Mission High School team in San Francisco.

An idea began to germinate shortly after my library visit. The next time we met at breakfast, I said to Wally just as I was leaving, "I have a proposition for you. Why don't we write a book together about baseball and life during the Twenties and Thirties? Don't answer me right now. Think it over and let me know in a day or two."

The next morning Wally was sitting at the counter. There were no vacant seats near him, so I waved to him and went to the opposite side. He nodded in return, and called out his laconic reply: "Let's do it!"

INTRODUCTION

Our book is a genuine collaboration. Wally and I taped our original discussions for fifty sessions. Over a period of months we edited and expanded the transcriptions. For the next nine years we had breakfast conversations several times each week. Wally proved to be extraordinarily spontaneous and articulate, and his memory for detail was remarkable.

We did library research at the Citizens' Savings Athletic Foundation, originally the Helms Athletic Foundation. (It is now sponsored by the Amateur Athletic Foundation of Los Angeles, a beneficiary of the surplus from the successful Olympic Games.) Here we enjoyed the hospitality of Wally's old friend, Bill Schroeder, Founder and Director, and his assistant, Braven Dyer, Jr. We want to acknowledge their help and support.

We also used a variety of original sources: scrapbooks compiled by Wally, letters, contracts, notices, photographs (Wally never threw anything away); and most important of all, Wally's eyewitness accounts of the baseball world in which he was both participant and observer for over two decades. The documentation of his bargaining with management which appears in the Appendix is, I think, unique in the history of baseball.

Wally's experiences and observations are the essence of the book. He is lucid, graphic, frank and objective. I must emphasize that he was never one to toot his own horn, nor does he ever manifest any false modesty. In his exchanges with management, this highly-intelligent, resourceful and independent high-school drop-out more than holds his own. As to who was the more logical, you be the judge.

At the beginning I didn't even know whether Wally had been a right-handed or left-handed hitter. After lengthy dialogue and extensive research, I became his enthusiastic advocate and eventually a close friend. The plan of the book and the background material were my responsibility. My evaluation of his career – his achievements and his place in the constellation of players in his own time and in modern baseball history – is based on the historical record. I toot Wally's horn and I toot it very loudly.

FOR EXAMPLE:

In 1936, Wally Berger completed his seventh year with the Boston Braves. In 1992, Barry Bonds completed his seventh year with the Pittsburgh Pirates. Bonds' salary for his seventh year was $4,700,000. Wally's salary for his seventh year was $12,500. Here is a comparison of their statistics for the seven years:

Name	Games	Runs	Hits	2B	3B	HR	RBI	BA
BONDS	1010	672	984	220	36	176	556	.275
BERGER	1017	637	1232	239	51	194	724	.304

In *The Hidden Game of Baseball* (1985), John Thorne and Pete Palmer fed baseball data into the computer in an attempt to evaluate players more effectively over time – to account for the previously unaccountable. I use their evaluations to compare Berger as a hitter with some of his contemporaries in the National League who made it into the Hall of Fame.

SLUGGING PERCENTAGE - LIFETIME:
(Numerical order in baseball history.)
Ott, 22; H. Wilson, 28; BERGER, 34; Klein, 37; Medwick, 44; Hafey, 52.

ON BASE PLUS SLUGGING PERCENTAGE - LIFETIME:
Ott, 16; H. Wilson, 29; BERGER, 45; Klein, 54; P. Waner, 64; Medwick, 70.

ISOLATED POWER - LIFETIME:
Ott, 16, H. Wilson, 18; BERGER, 25; Klein, 31; Hafey, 41; Medwick, 83.

ISOLATED POWER - SEASON:
(1933) BERGER, 37; (1927) H. Wilson, 70; (1944) Ott, 80; (1938) Ott, 83; (1930) H. Wilson, 85.

Special Note: Whenever we refer to the Braves, we mean the Boston Braves (known as the Bees from 1936 to 1939), not the migrants to Milwaukee or Atlanta. It was a whole new ball game once they left their native turf.

13

POCATELLO
1927

14

ONE

A PERSONAL NOTE

Who Was Wally Berger?

Who was Wally Berger? To Arnold Hano *(A Day in the Bleachers*, 1955), he was a "lesser-known hitter." Hano merely mentions Wally in describing Willie Mays' sensational catch of Vic Wertz' fly in the 1954 World Series:

"...I have seen such hitters as Babe Ruth, Lou Gehrig, Ted Williams, Jimmy Foxx, Ralph Kiner, Hack Wilson, Johnny Mize and lesser known but equally long hitters as Wally Berger...send the batted ball tremendous distances..."

"...the fly, therefore, was not the longest ball ever hit in the Polo Grounds, not by a comfortable margin. Wally Berger had hit the ball over the left field roof around the four hundred foot marker..."

Ken Smith refers to Berger in passing as being "part of the company" that Johnny Mize kept *(Baseball's Hall of Fame,* 1970). Stan Grosshandler calls him "A Forgotten Slugger of Another Era," *(Baseball Digest,* November, 1981). Joe Fall remembers him curiously in a nostalgic piece *(The Sporting News,* April 26, 1982).

Bucky Walter gives the home-town hero a headline in his column in the *San Francisco Examiner:* "Our Wally Berger Remembered – At Last." He goes on to say, "However, only Golden Oldies here remember Berger, a local sandlotter at old Southside Playground, now the site of the Hall of Justice." *(San Francisco Examiner,* September 12, 1983)

We observe the 50th Anniversary of the All-Star Game. Surprise! There on the tube is Wally Berger, center fielder for the National League in 1933. No mention that he was the outstanding center fielder in baseball that year, the All-America selection.

The ultimate display of ignorance by a sports writer is Harold Sheldon's article *(The Second Fireside Book of Baseball* 1958). The title of the article is "California Always Was in the Majors," with a subtitle confidently proclaiming, "With Assembled Proof, of Course." Sheldon discusses the great Joe DiMaggio and Ted Williams. Then he talks about "other notable swingers," listing a number of interesting, colorful and talented hitters. Berger's name is missing. Sheldon then includes other hitters "not as high, but noted for their long range hitting," such as Joe Gordon, Bobby Doerr, Bob Elliott, Dom DiMaggio, *et al.* Berger is still missing; perhaps he didn't qualify because he didn't move to San Francisco until he was five years old.

Modern fans can't learn about Wally's achievements if they just look at the bare-bones data in *The Baseball Encyclopedia* (Macmillan). But there is no excuse for professional baseball writers; they are supposed to do their homework. The kids who collect baseball cards know him. He got letters from them almost every week.

Walter Anton Berger was one of the greatest outfielders in baseball during the Depression Decade (1930-39), the period in which he performed in the National League. Although he was best known as a slugger, he was a superb outfielder. Here is the testimony of Pie Traynor, the Hall of Fame third baseman and manager of the Pittsburgh Pirates:

"The best ball player in the National League last season was Wally Berger of the Boston Braves, and not Chuck Klein in my opinion...Berger was the whole Boston Club. He is not only a great hitter, but he has developed into a wonderful outfielder, and some of the catches he made were sensational to say the least." (Interview, 1933)

Wally hit the ball as hard and as far as anyone who ever played, but he puts Babe Ruth in a special category because the Babe hit the long ball more often than any other hitter, and he didn't care who was pitching.

Wally's slugging percentage for ten years in the majors was .522 (*The Baseball Encyclopedia, 1979*). Only twenty-seven hitters in history have been higher. Coupled with this figure was his batting average of .300 for the same period. Fewer than three per cent of all players became members of the "three hundred club."

In the field, he tried for everything that came out there. In putouts per game and in total chances per game, he ranks in the top twenty – all time.

He said of himself that his throwing arm was adequate for the major leagues. It must have been, because on April 27, 1931, he had four assists in one game; no outfielder in the major leagues has done that since. Moreover, in a game at Pocatello in 1927, he had eleven putouts in one game in center field – including the last six outs of the game!

Boston sportswriter John Drohan, in his fifth year of "Berger Watching," made these observations:

"Like a prophet in his own country, Berger is often overlooked by local fans. This may be due to the fact that he does his work without fuss or feathers. He's such a long geared, speedy individual that he gets over the terrain with the speed of an antelope. Consequently, he is under fly balls that would force other outfielders to make spectacular catches if they reached them.

"...here is a youth who would hold his own in any day and age. And this includes such great center fielders as Tris Speaker, Ty Cobb and Hugh Duffy, generally classified as the greatest of all time.

"There isn't anything required of an outfielder that Berger can't do. He's sure as death on a flyball, can throw, and there have been several complaints that he can hit." (Column, 1934)

Wally was an excellent base runner, having been trained by a master of the art, Marty Krug, his manager in Los Angeles. Sportswriter Bob Bohne, writing in 1938, said, "Berger's long distance power centers all attention in his offensive, but few fans know that he was and still is one of the fastest runners on the circuit. Many men are faster going to first, because his hard swing puts him off-balance at the start, but when he gets steam up, he can really fly."

Because of his speed and skill on the bases, it might seem contradictory to report that he stole very few bases – a total of thirty-six in ten years – and thirteen of these came in his second year.

Not at all. His primary job was to drive in runs, and his manager for nine of his ten years was conservative Bill McKechnie. Bill did not call for the steal very often, especially in Boston. And the Thirties was not a base-stealing era. The leaders in the National League in that decade averaged under twenty-five stolen bases per season. Stan Hack, the leader in both 1938 and 1939, had a total of thirty-three for the two years.

Wally's personal history is as important to his evaluation as his professional achievements, and for it, too, he deserves to be freshly remembered.

Walter was born of German immigrant parents in Chicago in 1905. They moved to the Mission District of San Francisco in 1910. The story of his long struggle to get to the big leagues and his eventual success are the stuff of which the American Dream was made.

Horatio Alger, Jr., could have taken Wally's boyhood experiences whole for one of his dime novels. Wally was "Walt, the Newsboy" and "Walt, the Printer's Helper." He was also "Walt, the Bus Boy" at the famous Hotel Clift. Later he played semi-pro baseball for five years while working forty-four hours per week in a variety of jobs to help support his parents and family. Finally he was noticed by the San Francisco Seals, but it was a very circuitous route that led to the Pacific Coast League and then to the National League.

Wally often played the role of Frank Merriwell, the fictional hero of the stories of Burt L. Standish (William Gilbert Patten, 1866-1945). Merriwell always came through at the last moment to win the big game.

He was Merriwell so often that the fans always expected him to come through, or at least on the days when they came to the ball park. For example, he beat the Giants alone five times with his home runs in the season of 1930.

His most Merriwellian performance came in the last game of the 1933 season. Recovering from influenza, he was sitting on the bench when Boston began a rally. Bill McKechnie looked inquiringly down the bench toward him.

Weakened by the flu and wearing a "cold jock strap" (as the saying goes), he went up to bat with the bases loaded. He hit a home run to win the game and move Boston into fourth place. It was called a "ten-thousand-dollar" home run, because it meant that all the Braves would get a small piece of the World Series money. The *Spalding Guide* for 1934 recounts this dramatic finish. Al Hirshberg gives all the details in his book, *The Braves, The Pick and the Shovel* (1948).

Wally also had exceptional strength of character, demonstrated in his early years of struggle in San Francisco, and always in his tough-minded bargaining with management. He remained reasonable and courteous even when they were patronizing and sometimes insulting.

However, this strength was revealed most forcibly during the 1935 season. His play on a team that won only thirty-eight games – fewer than the Mets of 1962 (won 40, lost 120) – was unique in baseball history. It was an astounding statistical record. It displayed unmatched persistence, tenacity and dedication. Eddie

Hurley, a Boston sportswriter, summed it up in his column titled "The Unsung Hero of a Lost Cause:"

"The spotless finish streak of those Chicago Cubs, the romping repeat of the Detroit Tigers and Wes Ferrell's brilliant comeback may be entitled to their share of screaming type as some of the outstanding baseball achievements of the year, but how about our own Wally Berger, whose slugging club has refused to remain silent, in spite of the helplessness of the Braves all year?

"It may be thrilling as well as interesting that Hank Greenberg is having his biggest year with the Tigers and that other sluggers are enjoying the baseball atmosphere, but all of them are in the thick of flag races and have plenty of encouragement in making their conquests.

"Berger's case is altogether different.

"Down there in the baseball darkness with the Braves, Berger has remained in the thick of the home run race on his own courage alone...and his record for this season is all the more remarkable and entitled to more than passing mention. As the Braves stagger and stumble through the stretch to the welcome finish line with little more than feeble efforts in their hopes to chalk up a victory now and then, Berger has forgotten all about the ill fortunes of his teammates--and continued slapping the sphere to all corners of the various ball orchards of the league. And his record for homers this year just about overshadows and other, simply because of prevailing conditions. Few sluggers, there are, who could come through in the face of such handicaps as the Braves have faced all year. Yet Berger continues to pepper them and may keep it up right through to the finish."

The criteria for selection to the Baseball Hall of Fame, other than playing ability, are "integrity, sportsmanship, character, contribution to the team on which they played, and to baseball in general."

The deeper Wally and I got into our research the more I realized what an extraordinary player he had been. Although I knew that he had not yet been selected for the Hall of Fame, I was amazed to discover that he has been almost completely ignored by the Baseball Writers of America, and that he has been passed over year after year by the Special Veterans' Committee.

As to his integrity and sportsmanship, there can be no question about Wally's rating. He ranks with the best whenever and where ever he played. Ironically, this may be one of the reasons that he has been so thoroughly neglected – he was too well-behaved!

His contributions both to his team and to baseball were great. For seven years, he was the Braves' outstanding player and their biggest draw at the gate. Later in his career he helped the Giants and the Reds win National League championships. In every respect the cliche, "He was a credit to the game," applies to Wally Berger.

Why, then, the silence and lack of consideration? It would be an excellent topic for a thesis in sociology or social psychology by some enterprising graduate student. The brilliant social historian, Daniel J. Boorstin, provides some clues in his discussion of fame (*The Image: A Guide to Pseudo-Events in America,* 1982). Halls of fame are, for the most part, pseudo-events. There are now hundreds of them. Everyone is getting into the act; they are frequently promotional, self-serving or discriminatory.

Having said all this, one must admit that Baseball's Hall of Fame is the Phi Beta Kappa of professional baseball. It does signify merit; it does maintain high standards for admission. It lacks, however, an objective and predictable method of establishing the required grade point average for election.

In the case of Wally Berger, my own findings yield a number of possible explanations. FIRST, there is the business of personality. The truth is that "being a character" is more important than character itself. That is, being "colorful" is crucial in the minds of sportswriters. In fact, they often create characters. They invent nicknames. They play up characteristics of players in their creative columns. They encourage "characters" to continue to behave as characters.

The sportswriters reminded Wally of his deficiencies of character, but he was never able or willing to provide them with the kind of copy they wanted.

"Although naturally a trifle reticent, which means that Berger would rather sit back and listen than to 'pop off' too much, the young man is an interesting conversationalist when so inclined." (J. A. Kiernan, 1934)

"Berger hasn't possessed the color of a Ruth or a Cobb, but his close association with the Bambino may give him new enthusiasm for the game and teach him how to capture the public fancy in a greater degree than ever." (George C. Carew, 1935)

"Wally Berger, star of the Boston Bees outfield, is quiet, sincere, a great player, well liked by his league, by the press. He has a sly sense of humor and a God-given physique.

But Wally keeps his light hid under a bushel. It is one thing to be too gabby, it is another to forget that baseball is a game not only of hands and legs, but of color and box office. The big player should pay more heed to the dramatic elements of the game." (Sports editor – no byline, 1937)

SECOND, and closely related to the first explanation, was Wally's failure to acquire a humorous, catchy or memorable nickname. "I never got a nickname that stuck," says Wally. "The sportswriters tried 'Ham' and 'Biff' and 'Lim,' and some others that I don't remember. Actually I was always known as 'Walt' until the writers kept referring to me as 'Wally.'"

THIRD, there is the player's team standing in the league. It is important to be with a winner – or at least a contender. Boston was neither during Wally's tenure. He was, in the words of Eddie Hurley, "...down there in the darkness with the Braves." Writer Arthur Duffy summed it up in 1936, Wally's last full year with Boston:

"Berger is one of those ball players who has been forced to make his own way. One of the greatest athletes in the National league, he has never heard the plaudits of World Series crowds, or even come close, because as long as he has been with the club, the Bees have never been closer to a pennant than fourth..."

FOURTH, it helps to be a member of a "wrecking crew," that is, the heavy hitters who bat third, fourth and fifth in the lineup. The Braves never had one in the Twentieth Century – except for Berger, who was sometimes a one-man wrecking crew.

Contrast his situation with the RBIs of the sluggers on the Yankees' wrecking crew of 1936: Lou Gehrig (152), Joe DiMaggio (125), Tony Lazzeri (109), George Selkirk (107), and Bill Dickey (107). Moreover, the Yankees that year had seven regulars batting over three hundred.

FIFTH, there are the statistical comparisons which are often made as if all players on all clubs competed on even terms. In the Thirties, there were enormous differences in playing conditions from park to park.

There are still significant differences, but at least the dimensions of the playing fields have become more uniform as new

21

stadiums are built. Left-handed sluggers no longer have the advantage that they enjoyed in the parks of the Thirties. Baseball reporters and television critics are generally aware of these factors, but they seem to forget them when comparing Wally's statistics with those of his contemporaries who have been selected for the Hall of Fame.

Consequently, an objective analysis of all these data would validate, I believe, that Wally was the equal of any of the great National League outfielders now in the Hall of Fame who played in the decade from 1930 to 1939. These would include Cuyler, Hafey, Klein, Ott, Medwick, Wilson and the Waner brothers.

SIXTH, the Braves' financial situation was very poor – although owner Judge Fuchs paid himself very well and entertained lavishly. The coaches counted baseballs carefully, and at least one time they had to reduce an order for new bats. They paid players poorly, couldn't afford to develop a farm system and couldn't compete for the best prospects (They got Wally from the Cubs-owned Angels only because the Cubs already had a great outfield and wanted third baseman Lester Bell from the Braves). By the middle of the 1935 season, the Braves were broke and had to be taken over by the League until they were reorganized.

LAST, in the Berger case, there is a hidden psychological factor: Because Wally has been overlooked, he will continue to be overlooked. Because he has not been considered, he will not be considered. The case will not be opened, and prejudgment will prevail.

So there you have it.

Berger was modest, quiet, hard-working, conscientious and disciplined. He didn't throw tantrums, kick dirt on umpires, become involved in scandal or engage in wacky behavior. He didn't make good copy for the boys in the press box.

In his prime, he played in a "pitcher's park" with a team that never came close to winning all the marbles. It was a club out of the mainstream. It was inadequately financed, poorly administered, and usually overmatched on the field.

Despite all this, the Braves were always an interesting team, a team that had its great moments. They were led by the best manager of the times and supported by devoted and hopeful fans. And for seven seasons their most brilliant, courageous and persevering player was Walter Anton Berger.

The Greeks Had A Word For It: One of America's great

historians, Crane Brinton, in his *A History of Western Morals* (1959), borrowed a Greek word to clarify the nature and meaning of competition in human affairs. That word *agon*, which originally meant "the formal religiously-ritualized assembly of the Greeks to witness their games." Later, *agonia* came to mean any struggle, trial or danger with overtones of harshness and pain. From it comes the English word, *agony*.

Brinton uses *agon* to mean "the struggle for prize...the desire of men to gain honor and esteem by winning out in competition with their fellows, the need for ritual recognition of such achievement, the need for rules of the game, for a code in short, for morality..."

Professional baseball, despite all the changes in American social life since its beginnings, somehow retains these values. There is still the ancient struggle for prize. The most indulged, worldly-wise or cynical player feels its power. The ultimate prize "is not mere success, not mere leading of the league. Honor, in a curious way, is its own reward."

Wally Berger's career epitomizes this struggle. In his own time, on every level of play – from bush ball in the parks of San Francisco to the rarefied reaches of the Polo Grounds in New York – he was a competitor of the first rank, and he won the ultimate prize:

Honor.

TWO

BEGINNINGS

Wally's account of his boyhood play in San Francisco describes a world that has almost disappeared. Life was simpler then; kids just walked down the street to the ball park, got in free Friday afternoons and sat in the bleachers. They they could shout to their heroes and enjoy a friendly exchange.

Like Tom Sawyer and his friends, they planned and organized their activities themselves, in contrast to the experience of the "organization boy" in Little League today.

And a leader like Monk Amoroso always seemed to emerge to challenge any "nine to twelve-year-old team" by writing to "Bush Ball Bingles."

A. Bush Ball Bingles

When I was a boy around nine years old, I listened to my father talking about baseball. Before we moved to San Francisco, he ran a saloon in Chicago where old-time Chicago White Sox players used to come in and play cards. He told me their stories about the Chicago White Sox and the glories of the "hitless wonders" way back in 1905.

His telling me about all these characters aroused my interest in baseball. When I was in grade school, and this is going back to 1915, there were some kids in the school yard talking about the big leagues and the World Series. It was the Boston Red Sox and the Phillies. I kind of liked the Red Sox. It sounded good to me the Boston Red Sox. Well, I don't remember how they came out; I think the Red Sox won. (NOTE: Wally's memory is good. The Red Sox won in five games.)

To a kid it was like a fairy tale. In my imagination I pictured the Chicago team with Mordecai Brown, "Piano-Mover" Schmidt, and all the others I heard about. With penny candy you could get pictures of ball players like you do with bubble gum now. I'd pick up Hans Wagner, Ty Cobb or someone like that. In their uniforms

25

those ball players were like knights in armor to me.

Baseball got to be something I liked so much that I could play every day. I went to all the games I could and played on the streets and empty lots. I would imagine that I was in the big leagues, and that I was Joe Jackson of the White Sox when I was up there hitting.

I was living in San Francisco in the Mission District, near the Pacific Coast League park, which was located at 15th and Valencia. I went to school close by there, too. Friday was "kids day" when the Seals were playing at home. The games started at 3:00 in the afternoon, as there was no night ball then.

I'd cut class sometimes the last period on Friday to take in the games. Oh, it didn't happen every Friday. Only when the club was home – perhaps three or four times during the school year. Manual Training was the last class of the day. Mr. Dowling, my teacher, never called the roll. I thought, "Well, he's never going to miss me," and I'd take off.

It was worth taking the chance to see my San Francisco Seals. In the summertime there was no problem. On Friday afternoons, the bleachers would be packed with kids who got in free. The cops would have to keep an eye out for adults who might try to slip in.

Ping Bodie was probably my favorite player. He had been up in the big leagues with Chicago in the American League, and had come back down to the Pacific Coast League in 1915-16. Later, he went back up with Philadelphia and New York in the American League for five more years. When he came back to the Pacific Coast League, I played against him in 1928 or 1929. He was a native San Franciscan and was very popular as a home-run hitter.

I like outfielders, I guess. Justin ("Mike") Fitzgerald, a little fellow who could steal bases, was in right field. Ping Brodie played in center. In left field there was Biff Schaller, a good-natured guy who talked to the kids in the bleachers.

Biff was from Chicago. We were close to him in the bleachers, and he'd turn around and talk to us. We were always teasing him out there. He was well-liked, favored for being that way. His language was colorful, and along with his Chicago accent, he was a favorite character with the press and the fans. Biff was once quoted as saying, "The multitude is great in Salt Lake City – the ball will go a mile in that thin air." He made good copy for the sports writers.

1922 "CHAMPIONSHIP" BASEBALL TEAM

Capt. Flood   Cronin   Berger   Pence   Tejeda   Hollister   Anderson
(Coach)   Mitchell   Cooke   McDonald   Sheehan   Gallagher
                    (Manager)   (Captain)

They played him up similar to the way Dizzy Dean was played up in the thirties when he pitched for the Cardinals. (Both Fitzgerald and Schaller had very brief careers in the majors.)

When we started playing sandlot ball, we'd go down to some big empty lot. One I remember was on Army Street at Mission; we called it the Army Street Lot. We'd get a bunch of kids together and choose sides. We'd toss the bat and make a game down there. We fixed up the field ourselves with whatever material we could find. We played as often as we could after school and on Saturdays.

On my block was a boy named Monk Amoroso. He got a bunch of us together and we organized a team. We called ourselves the "Blazing Arrows;" I don't remember where the name came from, but we thought it was pretty good.

We used to advertise free in the evening paper in San Francisco. I think it was the *Daily News*. They had a column called "Bush-Ball Bingles." We'd write to 'em and say: "We challenge any nine to twelve-year-old team to a game. Call Monk Amoroso."

We could play at certain playgrounds in the neighborhood somewhere, and so we got started. We didn't have any uniforms didn't have any shoes! Some of us had gloves and that's how we got started there. I played like that until I went to high school.

B. Alma Mater, Hail and Farewell!
(We who are about to flunk, salute you!)

"...Joe Cronin was the star shortstop of the league with his great handling of all manner of hits through his position. Berger at third was the Babe Ruth of the league with his husky clouts and consistent fielding."
—*The Mission*, 1922.

In June, 1922, Mission High School won the championship of the San Fracnisco Athletic League. On page 72 of *The Mission* is the team picture. The yearbook also includes a commentary simply titled, "Baseball," from which the above quotations are taken.

In the back row of the picture, standing next to Captain Flood, were Joe Cronin, the shortstop, and Walter Berger, the third baseman. Captain Flood, looking very much like General Pershing in his World War I vintage uniform and his neatly trimmed mustache, was the assistant coach, who "loaned a helping hand to Mr. Chase and proved himself a real Missionite." Coach Robert Chase (also teacher of English, history and Latin), a former stroke on the crew at Yale, was missing from the picture. However, he did receive favorable comment on page 73.

In a newspaper summary of the season's play we get some indication of the state of the sport in a 1922 high school. "Lowell, perhaps, looked the best on paper. They were runners-up last year and have had practically the same team. They have also had the advantage of a regular coach this season – Knellin, formerly athletic director at Stanford, having taken over..." (Imagine, a regular coach!)

The first evaluation of Wally Berger to appear in the press was a report on the Poly game: "...Berger, the third baseman (Mission High) is about the best batter in the city schools. In the Poly game he got three clean hits out of five times at bat, with Hampton pitching. Hampton allowed only five hits to the whole Mission team on this occasion..."

Mr. Chase, my history teacher, was the baseball coach. Occasionally, when he was busy, Captain Flood, the R.O.T.C. Instructor, would take the ball club out. He was quite a fellow. Either Mr. Chase or he would be there because someone had to be in charge, but the boys would run the club. They knew more about the game than the guys who were supposed to coach us. For instance, they'd tell them when to bunt; they'd tell each other what to do.

We came from a working-class neighborhood. It was mainly German-Irish. We were all kind of poor and we all played baseball. The kids went to the ball park on Fridays and studied the game – believe it or not – they watched the good players. Then they talked about it. "Did you see that play? did you see what they did?" They'd see a double-play combination, and when they'd practiced it, they'd try the same thing. They were schooled pretty well in baseball and learned quite a bit from watching professionals.

In 1920 when I went out for the high school team, the coach said to us, "Those who have baseball shoes raise your hand." See, they didn't supply any shoes or equipment except the uniforms.

Well, I wanted to get that uniform, so I lied to the coach and said, "Yes, I got a pair of shoes." In fact, I had my eye on some to borrow. There was a fellow down the street from where I lived named "Muck" Fahey. I knew he had a new pair of shoes, so I said

29

to him, "How about borrowing your shoes for one game?"

He agreed – but I ended up keeping those shoes for the whole season! I was afraid to give them back, afraid I'd never get to use them again. I didn't make the team as a regular when I was a freshman, but the second year I did. In the meantime I got a pair of shoes, an old pair that some kid gave me. They had all kinds of patches on them, they had been mended so many times.

In my first season as a freshman, when I was a substitute (extra man), I remember we took a trip to San Mateo and the coach put me in right field. I was scared to death. "Here I am. I had the uniform on and I'm out in the outfield. I caught a fly ball. I was real proud of that; I caught it!"

By the next season, I had a year's experience playing sandlot baseball. I had matured enough so that I handled myself a lot better. I made the team and played third base all year. We played out at Golden Gate Park and South Side Playground (three diamonds) at 7th and Harrison Streets; we didn't have our own field. We didn't win anything that year in the City League.

In my junior year I played third again, but I went to work after school. My father frowned on me playing baseball – he thought I ought to help support the family. I got a job at Moise and Klinker's, a print shop in downtown San Francisco that made rubber stamps and did job printing. I was afraid to quit my job and play baseball, but the place burned down, so I had an excuse. I said to my father, "The shop burned down. I can't work there anymore. I'll look for another job." Instead, I went out for the team.

Sitting out on third base in my old position from the year before was Joe Cronin, who later played for the Washington Senators and became a Hall-of-Famer. I told him, "Joe, this is my place. I played here last year; you go over to short." So he went over to shortstop. But there was an Irish kid already playing at short, Joe Sheehan, and he didn't want to move: "Get out of here. This is my place. You go over to second." Somehow it turned out that Cronin finally played shortstop that year – and Sheehan did move over to second.

A word about our shortstop, Joe Cronin, because we were to play on opposite sides in the first All-Star Game at Chicago in 1933, eleven years later. I was in center field for the National League and Joe was at shortstop for the American. We were also both selected on the All-America Team of 1933, consisting of the best players in

30

both National and American Leagues.

Joe was our best infielder. He was good enough when he was about sixteen to play over in Napa with good semi-pros. It was a very fast team with some pros on it – professionals who had played in the lower minor leagues. They'd get a job somewhere and pick up an extra five or ten dollars playing on Sunday.

Author's note: Joe Cronin made it to the big leagues first (he beat Wally by four years, going up to Pittsburgh in 1926 when he was only twenty years old). Their paths crossed many times, the last time at the fiftieth anniversary of the All-Star Game at Chicago in 1983. Cronin made it big; by 1933 he was the Manager-Player for Washington. In 1935 he moved to Boston as manager and player.

Anyway, that year we won the City League championship. We finished the regular season in a tie with Poly and had to meet them in a playoff game which we won, seven-to-three.

But we almost didn't make it. Report cards came out and almost every member of the team flunked. The faculty wasn't going to let us play, but since Mission High had not won a championship since 1912, they had a meeting and decided, "We'll let them play on one condition that they come in after school and make up their studies." Well, most of us horsed around instead of studying, which was bad. We got to play that game, but I got left back.

Most of the other players were left back, too. I guess we were all in the same boat, but I decided to really bear down and catch up with my class. It was off-season, and I did bear down. Then my report card came out and I had flunked in history. My history teacher was the coach of the baseball team. I said to myself, "How can he give me a four or a five?" It was one, two, three, four, five see, five was a failure.

I went to him and said, "I got a one on my exam, my notebook was a one and I did everything else all right." He responded, "Yes, you did, but you didn't write the essay on Charlemagne."

"But I was working after school," I explained, "and I couldn't get to the library."

"Nevertheless," he replied, "until you make that up, you're a failure."

Well, I thought, if that's their attitude well, that's when I

Play by Play Account A.P. of Great Chicago Game

N 7-6-33 A.P.

First inning, National league—Martin grounded out, Cronin to Gehrig. Frisch went out the same way. Cronin made a fine running, one-handed catch of Klein's short fly. No runs, no hits, no errors, none left.

First inning, American league—Both managers shuffled their lineups at the last minute. Jimmy Wilson went to catch for the Nationals and Pepper Martin went to third. Chapman was thrown out by Martin. Gehringer was the first player to reach base, drawing a walk with a 3 and 2 count as Bill's slant zoomed in above his neck. The crowd roared as Ruth came to bat. After feeding the Bambino three straight balls, Hallahan got him with three straight strikes, the last one called. On the last strike Gehringer stole second. Gehrig was out, Terry to Hallahan, who covered first. No runs, no hits, no errors, one left.

Double Killing

Second inning, Nationals—Hafey's pop fly fell safe for a single back of second as Gehringer missed it after a hard run backwards. Terry hit the first pitch for a single to left, Hafey stopping at second. Berger lined to Dykes who threw to Gehrig to double Terry. Batrell struck out on three pitched balls, missing Gomez's curves by a wide margin. No runs, two hits, no errors, one left.

Second inning, American — Simmons flied high to Berger. Dykes walked. Cronin also walked, strolling on a count of four to one. The National league infield gathered about Hallahan as McGraw waved two pitchers into action in the bull pen. Rick Ferrell flied to Klein. Both runners stuck to their bases. Lefty Gomez drew first blood by slapping a hard single to short left centre, scoring Dykes. Cronin stopped at second. Chapman forced Gomez, Bartell to Frisch. One run, one hit, no errors, two left.

Third inning, Nationals—Dykes took J. Wilson's slow roller and threw him out. Hallahan got a big hand as he came to bat. Simmons made a fast dash to right centre to get Bill's high one. Cronin went back on the grass to get Martin's high pop fly. No runs, no hits, no errors, none left.

Babe Smashes One

Third inning, Americans—Gehringer drew another walk with a 4-1 count. Ruth, with the count one and one, hoisted one of Hallahan's slants into the lower right-field grandstand seats for a home run, scoring Gehringer ahead of him. The crowd gave the Babe a tremendous ovation as he doffed his cap and cantered around the bases with a wide grin on his face.

Eddie Collins, coach of the Americans, did an Indian dance as Babe strutted his specialty. Gehrig drew still another walk and Hallahan went to the showers. Out of the bull pen strode Lonnie Warneke, pride of the Chicago Cubs' pitching staff, to replace him. Hallahan had allowed three runs, two hits and five walks. Simmons hit into a lightning double play, Bartell to Frisch to Terry. Dykes singled sharply past Martin. Cronin flied to Berger. Two runs, two hits, no errors, one left.

Pulls Down Drive

Fourth inning, Nationals — Alvin Crowder, right-handed star of the Washington Senators, replaced Gomez on the mound for the American league. Simmons made a beautiful running catch in left centre to haul down Frisch's long drive. Klein tapped along the first base line and was out, Gehrig unassisted. Hafey fouled out to Dykes. No runs, no hits, no errors, none left.

Fourth inning, Americans—Rick Ferrell flied out to Klein in short right. Frisch tossed out Crowder. Martin threw out Chapman on a fast play. It was the first time the Americans had gone out in order. No runs, no hits, no errors, none left.

Fifth inning, Nationals—Gehringer threw out Terry. Cronin stopped Berger's hard smash and tossed to Gehrig, who made a stretching, one-hand catch to make the out. Bartell lifted a high foul to Gehrig who let it slip out of his glove. It was an error on Larrupin' Lou. The crowd gave him a big razzing but he got the same chance a minute later and hung on to the ball. No runs, no hits, one error, none left.

Fifth inning, Americans—The National league ball was now put into play and Bill Klem, dean of National league umpires, went behind the plate.

Berger Nabs Long Fly

Gehringer flied deep to Berger. Babe Ruth got another big applause and responded by dumping a short fly to centre field for a single. Gehrig struck out, swinging from the heels at the last strike. Simmons sent Ruth to second with a sizzling single past Martin. Dykes forced Simmons, Bartell to Frisch. No runs, two hits, no errors, two left.

Sixth inning, Americans—Gabby Hartnett, Chicago Cub backstop, went in to catch for the Nationals. Cronin singled past second. Rick Ferrell sacrificed and was out Terry to Frisch, who covered first. Earl Averill of Cleveland batted for Crowder. Averill singled through the box, scoring Cronin. Chapman caught the National infield asleep and laid down a perfect bunt along the third base line, making first easily as Martin stumbled after fielding the ball, Averill stopped at second. Klein made a fine catch of a long foul by Gehringer, and Averill had lots of time to make third after the catch. Chapman stayed on first. Ruth struck out as the crowd howled. One run, three hits, no errors, two left.

Seventh inning, Nationals—Lefty Grove of the Athletics took the mound for the Americans with his fire ball. Terry greeted him with a looping single to left centre. Berger forced Terry, Cronin to Gehringer. Pie Traynor of the Pirates batted for Bartell. Traynor delivered with a long double to centre that Simmons lunged at and just missed. Berger stopped at third. Hartnett, a notorious victim of Grove's slants in the 1929 World's Series, struck out. Woody English, Cub shortstop, batted for Warneke. English hit a high fly to Simmons. No runs, two hits, no errors, two left.

Hubbel on the Mound

Seventh inning, Americans—Carl Hubbel, Giant southpaw, took up the pitching for the Nationals, English replacing Bartell at short. Gehrig walked on pitched balls. Simmons forced Gehrig. Martin to Frisch. Dykes singled third, Simmons halting at second. Cronin fouled to Terry. Frisch threw Rick Ferrell. No runs, one hit, no errors, two left.

Eighth inning, Nationals—Martin called out on strikes. Frisch, batting right-handed, sent a hot grounder at Gehrig, but it bounded away from him with a freak hop for a single. Frisch flied deep to Simmons. Ruth leaned against the right field wall to make pretty catch of Hafey's long drive. No runs, one hit, no errors, one left.

Eighth inning, Americans—Paul Waner of Pittsburg went to right field for the Nationals, replacing Klein. Grove out, Terry, unassisted. Chapman at out. Hubbell was clipping the corner with a low, fast-breaking curve. Gehringer flied out to Berger. No runs, no hits, no errors, none left.

Ninth inning, Nationals—Sam Wes of St. Louis went to centre field, Chapman moved to right, and Simmons to third for the Americans. Gehringer threw out Terry. Chapman came in fast with a nice run to spear Berger's low drive. Tony Cuccinello of Brooklyn batted for English. Cuccinello struck out. No runs, no hits, no errors, none.

---

decided to quit school. I thought it was unfair. My teacher could have been a little more flexible about it. It was the same way with the other teachers, so I dropped out in my junior year. I decided I wanted to be a ball player, but I also believed I should go to work to help out with my family. I was reading about all those sixteen- and seventeen-year-old kids signing up. I was thinking that I was seventeen and I'd get a little bit of experience.

Then I went to see the Vice-Principal, Miss Goldsmith, and told her that I was going to go to work. Miss Ada Goldsmith was about fifty, I'd say. When you're in high school that seems old. Anyway, she had iron-gray hair and a sour puss. She looked at me with those cold eyes and said, "You know that you will have to go to part-time school until you're seventeen?" I was sixteen, then, I think.

"I have to work anyhow. We're a poor family and I want to help out at home."

She looked at me as cold as ever no sympathy at all and said, "Well, you're big enough to dig ditches, Walter!"

As I turned to walk out, I got in the last word: "Yes, Miss Goldsmith, maybe I could learn something about digging a ditch."

Later, the Board of Education sent a letter to my parents warning them that if I didn't report to school at least part-time, they would be fined. "Ma," I said, "don't worry; we haven't got the money anyway." They never followed up on their threat; I said the hell with them and went to work.

I didn't even go to the dinner they gave the baseball team. I didn't have any clothes to wear, just the cords that I wore to school.

I was out of school, but still very much interested in baseball. At one point I was about to give up baseball and concentrate on something else. I hadn't played for a few months when a fellow came up to me and said, "You want to play on Sunday? We're organizing a team for the San Carlos Athletic Club. Come on and play." I hesitated, but he urged me to give it a try. I went out and got started again playing on Sundays.

C. Pluck and Luck

Boys growing up during the Twenties were still reading the dime novels written by Horatio Alger, Jr., in the 19th Century. He wrote over a hundred of them they all had the same plot: the hero was always a poor boy who won fame and fortune by hard work, diligence, clean living, thrift and by being good to his mother. Luck was also an important ingredient. Our hero got the attention of a benefactor and often married his beautiful daughter. Of course, there were always temptations to which the hero never yielded.

Alger was a Unitarian minister who left the pulpit to become chaplain of the Newsboys' Lodging House in New York City and to take up a literary career. In addition to his novels, he wrote inspirational biographies of self-made men. Over twenty million copies of his books were published; they were read by generations of boys before radio and television. One of his most popular series was titled *Pluck and Luck.*

In many respects, Wally's struggle to make it to the big time was like an Alger story. He worked hard; he was self-reliant, diligent and thrifty. Above all, he was kind and helpful to his mother, and he *was* a newsboy! He persisted for five years, playing semi-pro ball and working just to make a living, until he got the attention of the San Francisco Seals.

When he got his first break with the Seals, bad luck pursued him in the form of an untimely back injury, and he had to wait another year. Finally his luck turned. A series of circumstances favored him, and he was on the road to fame and fortune. His fame proved to be greater than his fortune, which was, however, substantial for the times. And, on occasion, he had a benefactor.

Naturally there were exceptions in his career to the Alger myth. Wally hung around Kenealy's pool hall (a neighborhood institution which served important social purposes), a pastime that eventually served him well. Moreover, Wally always drank his full quota of beer during his playing days. Alger, of course, wouldn't have approved, but he would have admired Wally's pluck.

Wally was the oldest son of German immigrant parents who landed first in Chicago. His father, Anton "Tony" Berger, was born in Bavaria in 1881. His mother, Hedwig "Hattie" Steinke, was born in the same year. Wally was born in Chicago in 1905. The family migrated to San Francisco in 1910. By that time, there were three children all of whom rode West with Mother in a chair car, carrying with them a large basket filled with sandwiches. They settled in San Francisco's Mission District, where they lived in rented flats and moved frequently.

Wally had his share of luck good and bad as well as a good

supply of pluck. This Anglo-Saxon word is not much used today, but it is a handy noun. In the 19th Century it meant "courage" and "guts," and it still does today.

Coming from an Old-World German family, I learned to work. I was taught responsibility and discipline. My parents didn't baby me or take me anywhere. They were very strict, especially my father. He didn't have to say anything; he just looked at you and you knew what he meant. If my mother asked me to do something and I didn't jump to it, he turned around and said that I'd better get busy or he would get the razor strap. I quit one job to play baseball and he didn't like that. The next year, when baseball season rolled around, I had a job.

Another thing that I learned was thrift. We never wasted anything. When I was a teenager, I put money away. I paid my room and board as well, and when I went away to spring training my first time, I had money in my pocket. When I left for Butte, Montana, to play in the Miners' League, I had $100 in cash and my railroad ticket. Today that's not much money, but that amount went a long way then.

We were struggling in those days. In 1921 I made $25 a month working part-time at the Clift Hotel. In the summer I made $50 working full-time. I turned over every penny to my mother, who had to raise four kids. We had a big house and rented out a couple of rooms. My mother took in washing and ironing, and I used to make deliveries for her. It was a hard life and I helped my mother as much as I could. My father was gone quite a bit because he worked for the Matson Steamship Line and was off to Hawaii for weeks at a time.

In fact, my father and I weren't too close. He never took me to ball games like some fathers do. He was born in Bavaria and worked as a bar waiter and saloon-keeper in the Swiss Alps before coming to America. He was sort of a linguist because he had to know three languages, French, Italian and German, in order to work there. He had a saloon in Chicago before we moved to San Francisco, and he had a couple of cheap saloons in San Francisco. One was called *The Bismarck.*

My mother came from Prussia, from a little town on the Polish border. I didn't know that until one time when she was visiting Chicago and I was playing there with the Braves against the

Cubs. We went out to my grandmother's place where I heard my mother speaking Polish to one of the neighbors.

"Mom, where did you learn Polish," I asked. Her reply, "When I was a child, I went to school near the Polish border. We had to be able to speak both languages." I'm proud to say her Polish was pretty good.

My job at the Clift Hotel was a good experience; I learned a lot and I ate a lot. In 1921 the Clift was a classy hotel—it's still there and it is still one of the best hotels in The City. During school, I would work the 6-to-9 shift except when I was playing baseball. Then I would swap shifts with a bus boy who worked from 9 to midnight. In the summer, I worked full-time, which meant three meals: 6 to 9 in the morning, 12 to 3 in the afternoon and 6 to 9 in the evening. It was a long day, but between shifts I could go to the movies.

I also learned to wrestle while working at the Clift. One of the waiters, a wrestler on the team at U. C. Berkeley, taught me to wrestle at the YMCA where we had afternoon workouts. He was a middleweight and I had jumped to 175 pounds eating all those good meals at the hotel. He taught me all the holds. He was fast and good. It was speed in wrestling, you know you have to be quick. It was a good way to get exercise between shifts.

My experience at the Clift Hotel was important for me later on when I traveled on the road with baseball clubs. Most baseball players came from small towns and rural areas, but San Francisco was always a cosmopolitan city and the Clift was one of the best hotels. While I worked at the Clift, I learned how to dress, how to order in the hotel dining room, how to use the right fork and how to tip.

The hotel management and the guests were high-class people; what I learned from watching them gave me confidence. It also made me aware of how important tips are to workers in hotels and restaurants. Many ball players used to embarrass me with their low tips, and sometimes they wouldn't even leave anything at all for the services they received. They weren't deliberately crude, but they were trying to save money and they didn't understand how things really worked.

Mr. Clift, the owner of the hotel, had his breakfast every morning in the dining room. I think he lived at the hotel, and when his daughter got married, he asked me to help carry the champagne. They had a storage room downstairs in the basement full of wine, champagne and booze. I was the young guy assigned to carry up the bottles. (The Redwood Room had a bar before Prohibition, but all they served in 1921 was near beer.)

I became good at my job. Working with the waiters, I would see that patrons' glasses were always filled with water. Sometimes I would set the tables; you had to lay out the silverware knowing the right order and which side the knives and forks were on. They had butter dishes and there was a butter knife which had to be placed right. I'd also bring in the salads.

Not only did I become good, but I became a showoff. There were two flights of stairs from the dining room down to the kitchen. I would stack up a tray and hold it high over my head. I always ran until one day when I was carrying a box full of very expensive glassware, I caught my heel on one of the stairs and fell right in the middle of the kitchen. The Chinese glass washer (they even had a man to wash all the special glasses they used) screamed at me in Chinese I don't know what he called me, but it wasn't good. I think I slowed down after that.

The hotel waiters were all men, no women, and they had all worked there for years and years. They made two-and-a-half dollars a day, but they mainly depended on tips to make a decent living. Tips were often ten cents, or maybe two bits. How important they were became clear to me when I worked a dinner with Mr. Endert, the fellow who got me the job. Endert was called "Kewpie" because he had a big, round face and curly hair up in front of his balding head, which made him look like a kewpie doll.

One day, Kewpie had a businessmen's luncheon for about twenty-five people. The head waiter wanted to give him another waiter, but he said, "No, I can handle it if you give me that bus boy right there" pointing at me. We served them and when we were all through, the guy who paid gave him a one-dollar tip; we served twenty-five people and all we got was one silver dollar!

I watched Kewpie do something he shouldn't. Angrily, he said, "I was gonna give the bus boy that much," and he threw the silver dollar to me. He was censured by the head waiter because you are not supposed to do that even if the guests walk out without tipping. I figured that he should have got at least five dollars for twenty-five people; he had worked hard. That would have made his day. In addition to his two-and-a-half wages, the five would have made seven and a half for the day, a decent wage for a day's work.

That summer at the Clift, they had a chef named Hayes. He was a great big, heavy-set Irishman who liked me. When the cooks all sat in the kitchen and had their lunch, they had their choice, and they would say to me, "Sit down, kid." We really had the food – pork chops, roast beef, everything. I had lunch with those cooks all summer long. Hell, I gained twenty pounds and acquired a taste for the best.

Before I went to high school, I delivered the San Francisco *Chronicle* in the Glen Park area. In high school, after the bus boy's job at the Clift, I worked at Moise and Klinker, a printing firm. As mentioned elsewhere, this business burned down, giving me an excuse for not working during the 1922 season when I played on the championship team at Mission High.

After dropping out of Mission High, I had a variety of jobs while I was playing semi-pro ball and trying hard to get into organized baseball. In addition to being a carpenter's helper, I worked for about a year on the waterfront at Pier 42. I stenciled cargo for the American President Lines' boats, the *President McKinley* and others. We used symbols to indicate the contents, since the crews unloading the ships in the Far East couldn't read the lettering. I made fifty cents an hour, working five-and-a-half days (everybody worked at least a half-day on Saturday), and made twenty-two dollars per week.

For a couple of years I drove a truck and glazed French doors for the Nicolai Door Company. They let me take the truck home, and I'd stop at one of the parks for my workout. When I gave Nicolai notice the year I first went to spring training, my boss, Mr. Herring, said that they were planning to make me a shipping clerk. I had learned to handle all the business forms. It was a good promotion he was offering: forty-five dollars a week and a white collar, but baseball came first. I wasn't tempted; I went north to Boyes Hot Springs (near the town of Sonoma) with the Seals.

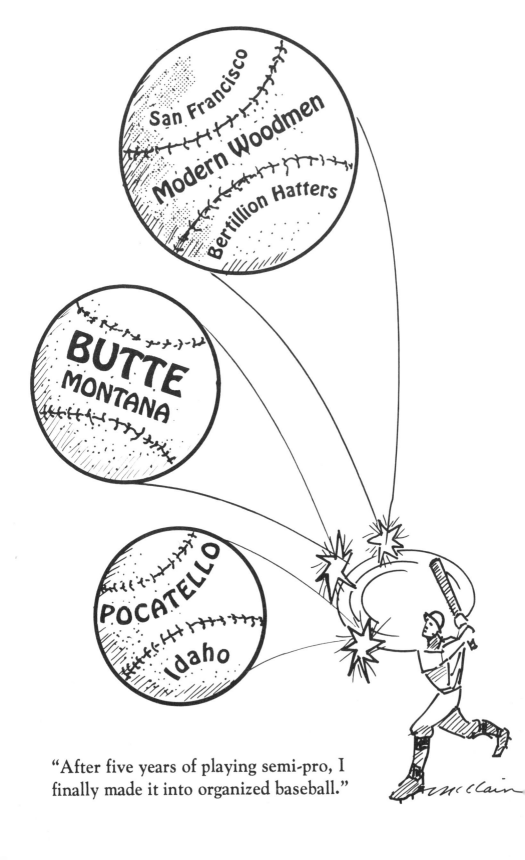

"After five years of playing semi-pro, I finally made it into organized baseball."

THREE

APPRENTICESHIP

A. Semi-Pro in San Francisco

In the beginning I played a few games with the San Carlos Athletic Club. In semi-pro ball, the team is always changing. You add a guy, drop a guy, and some guy quits and moves away. I stayed with that bunch of boys that summer and we wound up playing for the Modern Woodmen of America. We were pretty good and we played good teams all over the Bay Area.

The leagues were pretty loosely organized. We played only on Sundays and we didn't have professional people helping. The manager of a semi-pro team didn't know any more than the players. All he did was to get us together and say, "There's going to be a ten o'clock morning game at Southside Playground," and we'd all show up.

We just agreed among ourselves on the positions we'd play most of the time. However, under the conditions of play that existed, the outfield was considered least important. We played only on Sundays; we had to work during the week. I worked out after work as often as I could.

Most of the time I had to play the infield at shortstop or third base. I always asked the manager to put me in the outfield and he would always reply that he couldn't get a shortstop. And he'd say, "Well, I'll tell you, you play there until we find somebody."

When they finally got somebody to play there, he wouldn't come up to their standard, and then I'd be back at short again. I even got stuck at short when I went to play for Butte, Montana. Finally I got to play in the outfield at Pocatello. Even at Boston, McKechnie was thinking for a while about playing me at third base.

In San Francisco, they used to have these playgrounds that were scheduled solidly on Sundays. Southside Playground, for instance, had three diamonds, and each diamond had three games scheduled, a total of nine games on a Sunday. I always liked to play at the field at 7th and Harrison, because it was the most important in San Francisco – it even had stands for the spectators.

When we played for the Modern Woodmen, the members

41

of the lodge were very good to us. They made us all social members and allowed us to use their hall where they had games and pool tables. They enjoyed us, and we had a place to hang around. They provided us with uniforms and equipment. The uniforms were dark blue with pin stripes, somewhat like the traveling uniforms of the Chicago White Sox way back, or the Portland Beavers of the Pacific Coast League.

When we played in San Francisco, members of the lodge would come out to see us play. It was a kind of advertising, too, for the lodge. They would get their name in the paper every week. The game would be reported along with the box score, and they would be listed in the league standings in the Independent Winter League: 'Getting off to a flying start, the Independent Winter League, spreading its games to every playground diamond in the city, entertained a great number of fans yesterday.'

We all liked to get in a little travel, to go some place on a Sunday, and have a little adventure. Sometimes we played in places like San Rafael, Novato, Petaluma and Healdsburg. We didn't venture too far, but we did play in Vacaville and Pleasanton. Usually we got to games in a car borrowed by someone on the team. Often they were beat-up jalopies like a 1920 Chandler or something like that. Most trips didn't go too far, so we didn't have to worry about mechanical problems.

However, once we did make a trip up north some distance, and of course this time we *did* have trouble. We went to Point Arena by way of the Coast Route along Highway 1 with nine guys in the car. We had flat tires and had to add water to the radiator every fifteen miles. It took us a long time to come and go.

That night, we missed the last ferry from Sausalito back to San Francisco and had to sit in the car waiting for the ferry until early the next morning. We almost froze on that dock! I went right home, changed my clothes and went to work. No sleep at all, but when you're young, you can handle it.

B. Back and Forth with the San Francisco Seals

It began to look as if no one was going to look at me or give me a tryout in organized ball. There were no scouts following high school baseball the way they do now. There were old-timers who would follow the semi-pro teams and give tips to the management of minor league clubs. They were called 'bird dogs.' They were hang-arounds, guys who hung around the ball park and occasionally tipped the general manager that there's somebody out there. He might send someone around to take a look. Just when I was about to give up on the idea, I got a message from Charlie Graham, general manager of the San Francisco Seals.

In the Summer of 1925, the Modern Woodmen played a game against Mill Valley. A young pitcher named Eddie Oliva was pitching for Mill Valley for the summer; he had already been signed by the Seals to report the following spring. Against Oliva I had three for three, including two home runs. Reading the semi-pro page in the San Francisco *Chronicle*, Graham saw that I got three hits off his boy up there. He asked the clubhouse boy, a kid named Casey, if he knew me. Casey said that he knew me and could get in touch with me. Graham told him to bring me down to the office.

The first question Mr. Graham asked when I got to his office was, "How old are you?" I answered truthfully, "I'm nineteen; I won't be twenty until October." He didn't believe me. "Come on," he said, "don't give me your baseball age." What he meant was that he thought that I was cheating on my age, saying that I was younger so that later on I could say I was 31 when I would really be 35. I knew that ball players did that in order to get in a few more years. "No," I said, "that's it."

Mr. Graham then said, "Okay, I've got a contract here. Would you like to sign a contract and go to spring training with the Seals?" "Yes, sir," I said. I didn't even care to read it, although I did see that it was for $250 a month. I put my name on it right away. And they never even saw me play. On the strength of the box score, they signed me to a contract.

I later found out that it wasn't going to hurt them any. They signed me for $250 a month, then took eighty of us to spring training. After one week they dumped forty of them. It was a big wholesale thing – what could they lose? A little bit of room and board for a week or two.

Then in February, 1926, on the day before I was to leave for spring training, I hurt my back. I was working out at the Southside Playgrounds near the corner of 7th and Harrison (the freeway goes over this location now). There was a fence quite a distance out, and

I was up there in batting practice trying to hit it. I hit one a mile, but I swung too hard while I was turning. We played a game that afternoon and as I swung at a ball, something popped up there high in the back. I thought it was just a muscle, but I was a little worried.

That night, before I was supposed to leave, all the players on the semi-pro team that I played with (the Modern Woodmen) came down to my house. They tried to help me. Joe Sheehan, whose uncle, Mr. McTigue, had a stable at Army and Mission, brought some Columbia horse liniment. They rubbed my back with it; it really burned. I was hoping it would work, but I later discovered that I had pulled out a vertebra, and no amount of liniment was going to do any good.

The next morning the guys saw me off. With all the other players, I steamed north on the *Bullet,* the nickname for the local passenger train that took us to the Seals' training camp at Boyes Hot Springs. It was an ancient day coach, moving at a rate of at least 25 miles per hour.

When I got to camp, I saw Denny Carroll, the trainer. I had gotten to know him by hanging around the ball park. He worked on me a little bit, but I didn't get any better; so they gave me my release, recommending that I see a chiropractor in San Francisco. It was back on the *Bullet* to Sausalito.

Back home I told my Mother that I needed to go to a chiropractor. When I said that I didn't have any money to pay for treatments, she thought a moment and said, "You go to Doctor Shiller on Fillmore Street; he'll give you credit. You can pay him whenever you go back to work and get some money."

Dr. Shiller was a big German chiropractor. As he was bouncing around on my back, he said, "You've pulled your vertebra up and over a little bit. You've hurt it pretty bad. I don't think you'll ever play baseball again." He worked on me and got it back into place. It was swollen and I took hot baths with Epsom salts. The swelling went down after about ten treatments at two dollars a treatment. (At the time, I was making fifty cents an hour back at my old job at the door company.)

For quite a while, my back was weak. I was a little afraid of it; in fact, I was really downcast. I thought that Shiller might be right. About a month later, I went down to watch my old team play. A foul ball came my way and I automatically tossed it back. Nothing happened. So I started some light workouts. As I got my confidence back, I started swinging and throwing a little bit harder. I was ready again. I played with a fast semi-pro team, the Bertillion Hatters, and the Seals re-signed me for the next year.

With the Hatters in the San Francisco Winter League, I made five dollars a game. It was the first time I ever made any money playing baseball. I was surprised when they handed me the money – I didn't realize that we got paid. It was a fast league and we drew good crowds. For example, Max Kofskey reported in the San Francisco *Chronicle*: "Pete Maloney's Bertillion Hatters are the team to beat for the championship of the San Francisco Winter League. They proved it Sunday before a crowd of 2,000 by beating the Cottrell Brothers team, 3 to 1, in the feature attraction at Recreation Park."

Pete Maloney was our manager. They called him "Mugsey of the Bushes" after Mugsey McGraw, but not to his face. Like McGraw, he'd fight you if he heard you call him that. The team was made up mainly of pros no higher than 'A,' which meant no higher than a Southern League or a Texas League ball player and down to the 'D's.'

The Bertillion Hatters, our sponsor, had their store downtown at Sixth and Market Streets. We wore black uniforms with white socks with a black ring. Our shirts carried the Hatter's name. We were walking billboards, you might say. Thousands of people saw us play, and reporters who covered the games got their bylines in the paper. It was good publicity for the Hatters.

We were playing only once a week, which tended to make our batting averages not so sharp. Scores were frequently low: 2 to 1, 3 to 2, 1 to nothing, and so on. I played second base for the Hatters, even though I had played third in high school and shortstop with the Woodmen – all the inside positions. I wanted to be an outfielder all the time, but I was a good infielder, and that's where they tried to keep me. At the time, I told them I might grow too big for shortstop.

On the strength that my back was all fixed up, San Francisco signed me again. I quit my job again in February, 1927, and rode with another eighty or ninety fellows on the *Bullet* to Boyes Springs. This time I lasted two weeks.

We lived at a place called Peter's French Resort, where the sleeping rooms were little wooden shacks about nine-by-twelve. They used to double up the guys, two to a room. Two of you slept on an iron bed with a hard mattress. And there was no heat, even though it gets cold up there at that time of year. I slept with Lefty Tomasich, a guy who lived in my neighborhood.

However, they did feed us well. It was farm-style with long tables, two of them, and they just brought out the food and put it on the table. We helped ourselves. I was young and had a good appetite. That meat and gravy and mashed potatoes tasted good to me.

The Seals weren't interested in the position I played. They were mainly interested in how I could hit, then they would put me somewhere. I played first base as well as the outfield.

The second week I was there, Walter "Duster" Mails announced that he was ready to pitch. He was a left-hander that I had seen pitch in the Coast League. He was very fast; I had to bat against him. I grabbed a Tony Lazzeri bat and said to myself: "I'm going to have three good cuts off of him. It's no disgrace if he strikes me out." I guessed a fast ball and I was right. I got a hold of it and drove it a country mile over Lloyd Waner's head in left field. (There were no fences out there; it was just a big pasture. They just scraped out the place for their training grounds.) I scored before Waner even came up with the ball.

After I crossed the plate, Mails said to me, "If you play twenty years, you'll never hit one that far again." I thought he was kidding, so my next time up I guessed for the curve. See, I was starting to guess already. He *did* throw a curve and I singled through short. I felt good – two hits off a former major league pitcher.

Strange as it may seem, I got released that night. Manager Nick Williams called me in and said, "I have to cut down; I have to give you your release. Go back to San Francisco and wait until we break camp, then come and see me. I'll try to find something for you."

C. Butte by Way of Kenealy's Pool Hall

Nick Williams called me when he got back to the city. Nick liked me and had been trying to get me a job. He said, "I wired Bill Speas in the Mississippi Valley League, but he said that Berger has no record and he didn't want to gamble the fare on you."

"Nick," I asked, "How can a ball player get started? Here you're recommending me to a 'D' League team and the manager doesn't want me because I have no record in baseball?" Nick

46

replied, "I'm sorry about that. However, I can get you a job in Emmett, Idaho. It's like semi-pro; they don't pay much, but if you go up there and hit some home runs and do pretty well, they pass the hat and you can pick up $10 or $15 a game sometimes."

I said, "No, Nick, that's independent ball. I want to get into organized baseball." I didn't want to go to one of those small towns where you wear your uniform, wear the glove on your belt, and they've got you jerking sodas and they take up a collection when you're the town hero. I was about ready to see about that shipping clerk's job.

My dobber was really down when suddenly I got a wire from Harry Meyerson, who had been at Mission High. He didn't play on the high school team, but played on some pretty good semi-pro teams in town. He was in Butte, Montana, which was not organized ball. The manager asked Harry if he knew an infielder in San Francisco, and Harry recommended me. I don't know why. We barely knew each other, but he remembered that I was a long ball hitter. He sent the wire to me in care of Kenealy's cigar stand and pool hall on 14th and Valencia Streets.

Harry knew the message would get to me at Kenealy's. The Kenealy brothers ran this cigar stand and pool hall next to the Seals' park. (In those days, the Seals played at Recreation Park, at the corner of 15th and Valencia.) They knew everybody in town. All the ball players used to stop by. I lived near there and hung out there. The message got to me right away.

(I played against the Kenealy Team in the Mid-Winter league. I remember one game against them in particular. We beat them 15-1 and I hit a home run. It was unusual to have a high score like that, and home runs were pretty scarce when you played only once a week.)

The offer from Butte, Montana, was from the Anaconda Copper Company Team. It was a *miners'* league, not to be confused with the *minor* leagues. They wanted me to play shortstop, offering $275 per month. I wired back my acceptance, but I told them that I wanted transportation both ways. They agreed and I got a round-trip ticket to Butte by way of Salt Lake City.

It was my first time away from home. There was snow on the mountains at that time of the year in Montana. I was on my way! I felt great.

On the way to Butte, I had an hour layover in Pocatello,

Idaho, at six o'clock in the morning. Pocatello had a team in the Utah-Idaho League, which later became the Pioneer League. I knew a couple of guys from San Francisco on the Pocatello team, Jimmie O'Connell and Harry Benjamin. I found out that they were staying at the Bannock Hotel. In my enthusiasm, I went up to their room a little after six in the morning and knocked on their door. They mumbled that they were sleeping, but I woke them up and told them proudly that I was going to Butte to play ball. They replied, "Good luck," and rolled over to go back to sleep. I got back on my train and left Pocatello. (But not for long – I was back there in about two weeks or so.)

Coming into Butte, I saw all that red rock – not a tree in sight. It was a desolate place. I was heading up the hill with my cardboard suitcase toward the Hotel Finlen, when I happened to meet Harry Mayerson, the Butte player who had recommended me. He asked where I was staying. I pointed to the Finlen. "You don't want to stay there – that's eight dollars a day. Come on with me, we stay at the Central Hotel for a dollar a day."

In Butte, I was supposed to work for the mining company as well as play on their team. The first thing I was asked was, "Do you want to go down in the mine?" I answered quickly, "No, sir, you're not getting me down there. Give me a job on top." (I was thinking about the four miners who had been killed at the Bell Diamond Mine when a cable broke.) They gave me a job delivering air and water hose to the shop. The mules had been doing this chore for so many years that all I had to do was sit up in a chair on the wagon, let them drive it up to the shop and back up. Then I unloaded the hose.

After a few days, the timekeeper told me, "Why don't you go out and practice? You practice and I'll sign you in and out." I had to have a time card because I was on the Company payroll. After the first week, we didn't work any more. We practiced and played every Saturday and Sunday, and also some twilight games during the week.

Twilight games were scheduled for 5:30 or 6:00, and the miners would come right out of the mines with their lights on their caps. That was our crowd. It was entertainment for the miners. There were three clubs in Butte and another 25 miles away in the smelter town of Anaconda. Attendance was pretty good; there wasn't much else to do in town except gamble or drink. Mostly men

48

came to the games. There were very few women. The men were rough characters who yelled at us in pretty foul language.

One afternoon in Butte, I picked up a Salt Lake newspaper. Reading the box scores, I saw that a fellw named Vusich from Los Angeles had made five errors in one game playing in the outfield for Pocatello. I thought, "My God, I never made five errors all season! How did he get a job up there?"

It was quite a coincidence that a day later I got a wire from my friends Benjamin and O'Connell, asking how much I wanted to play the outfield for Pocatello. I'd just been benched by the Butte manager--which of course I didn't appreciate – and also I had not wanted to play the infield for some time, anyhow. So I jumped the Butte club and went to Pocatello for $200 a month, $75 less than I was making at Butte, but at least it was organized baseball.

I wasn't tied down at Butte. When I accepted the terms by wire to play in Pocatello, it was a contract. After five years of playing semi-pro ball, I had finally made it into organized baseball and was playing in the outfield, which had always been my preference.

D. Pocatello by Way of Butte

Wally Berger entered the records of baseball history in *Spalding's Official Base Ball Guide for 1928*. This statistical bible of base ball ("baseball" was two words in 1928 and for some years afterward) recorded data on every team, league and regular player in organized base ball in 1927. The *Guide* also contained twenty-four pages of information about college base ball, including schedules and pictures.

There is a picture, for example, of little Hiram College's thirteen-man squad, along with their coach, G. H. Pritchard. Hiram played a total of six games, two of which were with Akron. Franklin and Marshall College in Pennsylvania played nine games. The U. S. Military Academy defeated them 45-0 in one game and Ursinus did the same in another, 32-7.

The *Guide* also attached the "Official Base Ball Rules for 1928" with explanatory notes "In Convenient Detachable form for Ready Reference." All this for thirty-five cents.

The summary for the Utah-Idaho League is found on pages 278-282. The team in Pocatello for whom Wally played was known as "The Bannocks," after an Indian tribe which once lived there.

The other teams in the league were Idaho Falls, Ogden, Salt Lake City, Logan and Twin Falls.

The *Guide* reported that "the batting championship of the league was divided between Walter Berger of Pocatello and John Schinski of Logan." Wally was listed above Schinski with the identical average of .385 because his was a minute fraction higher.

Moreover, his total hitting performance exceeded that of Schinski. His slugging percentage, not computed nor listed by the league, was a hundred points higher than that of his rival. Runs Batted In were not given, but in total bases, Wally was in first place with 248 in 92 games (Schinski had 214 in 101 games). Wally broke the previous home-run record of twenty by hitting 24. Caffey of Salt Lake was second with fifteen. In fielding, Wally made 223 putouts in 92 games, the most of any outfielder. McCauley of Ogden had 221 in 96 games.

It was an impressive beginning for Wally. Los Angeles of the Coast League was impressed and brought him up for the last two weeks of their season "for a look." They kept him, and his record was to continue in the *Spalding Guide* for another twelve years.

I joined the Pocatello Club on the road in Idaho Falls. Since I was new, I didn't have a roommate yet. I heard the players in the next room talking about me. 'Who is that big guy from Butte?' one player asked. Another guy says, "His name is Walt Berger. He's from San Francisco."

The player that I was going to replace – the one who made five errors in one game – announced, "Wait 'till he plays that sun field out there and then see what he can do." Later on, when I would meet him, I'd remind him about what he said in that hotel room, and he would always deny saying it. He played afterwards with the Hollywood Stars, despite his bad experience with Pocatello.

He was right about that sun field. I hadn't often played right field and I didn't play it too well, but I hit a few right away. I started off in a double-header at Idaho Falls with four hits, and the manager, Ivy Olson, told me, "You're just the man I want."

However, a short time later, I did something wrong in right field and he stopped the game to move me to center field, where I stayed the rest of the year. That right field must have had Olson frustrated. The previous fielder had made seven errors in seven games, with a total of seven put-outs.

But I must have had *one* good day! All I remember is that I was really pooped, and I thought that if another damn ball comes out here, I'll never get it. It wasn't until I read the United Press story in the paper that I realized how busy I had been: *Pocatello, Idaho – August 9. What is believed to be a record in putouts for an outfielder was made here Friday by right fielder Berger of the Utah-Idaho League. Berger caught eleven drives to the outer garden during the game with Idaho Falls and had one assist, many of the chances ranging into the spectacular. He made the last six putouts of the game.*

The caliber of baseball in the Utah-Idaho League was pretty high. The Coast League clubs would send up their prospects to the six teams in Utah and Idaho, and as a result, they'd get the cream of California playing there. Off hand, I can remember fellows like Lombardi, Gomez, Camilli, Vergez and Daglia, who came out of the U-I League.

We got players who should have been playing in Class "B" or "A" ball. Los Angeles, for instance, had a working arrangement with Pocatello. I can remember at least a dozen guys who went up to the big leagues out of that league a couple of years later.

Our weekly schedule was just like the Pacific Coast League's, but the season was shorter – only about a hundred games on the average (Pocatello played 98). We didn't play double-headers on Sunday. We played six days and took Mondays off. We often used that Monday to travel on a bus to the next town on the schedule.

One big difference was the number of players. We had only fourteen, including the pitchers, who were extra utility players. The manager also played. Olson had played fourteen years in the majors and was in two World Series with Brooklyn. He had been a good shortstop in the majors. With Pocatello in 1927 he played mainly at first base and third. At age forty-two, he didn't do badly. He played in ninety-one of the ninety-eight games, batted a respectable .279, fielded .985 in sixty-one games at first and stole four bases.

Olson was a very tough manager – he rode his players and he rode me. He was a driving kind of person who made everyone mad at one time or another. He used to be on our necks all the time. He was just two years out of the majors, and this job in the 'D' league didn't pay much. I guess he wanted to stay in baseball and hoped to move up. I think he managed the year before in the Florida State League.

A good example of Olson's attitude was his lack of concern for his players. I pulled a charlie-horse, a pulled muscle in my leg, and went to the doctor for it. When he completed his examination, he told me, "You're going to have to take off a couple of weeks for that to heal. As long as you keep playing, it's not going to get any better." "Tell that to the manager," I replied, sarcastically. He shook his head and said, "You tell him that I said it won't heal unless you stay off it for a couple of weeks." I told Olson what the doctor said. His answer was, "You've got to play. We don't have any extra men."

I said, "All right, but don't run me." He wanted to use the hit and run to get me going. I repeated, "Don't run me." The next time I got on first he gave me the hit-and-run sign and I didn't go. I didn't miss the sign; I just didn't run. We got doubled up. He ran right down to first base, down the right field line, jumped on the fence, hung on, and then fell limply to the ground. He did it to show me up.

Olson rode me all season, but I fought back. One time when I was in scoring position, I just barely made it home. I didn't have any spring in my leg – it was dragging. I didn't slide into home and just beat the throw. Olson got on me about that: "There's a scout in the stands and you come home standing up?"

I defied him and answered, "You know what you can do with the scout." I played in pain all season, but I didn't give a damn. I was hitting good and I played half-mad most of the time. I heard that Ty Cobb played that way. I led the league in hitting and in home runs. They didn't keep records on RBI's, but I did all right there, too, I think.

The record book shows that I tied with Johnny Schinski of Salt Lake. We both hit .385, but when they carried it out another few digits, I beat him out. That winter, I happened to run into him in a sporting goods store, and we got into an argument about it, so just between ourselves, we tossed for it. I beat him on the first toss. Then he wanted it two out of three. I beat him two out of three, so I led the league both ways!

After Pocatello I saw Ivan Olson just three times. A few years later when I was with the Braves, we played in Macon, Georgia. Brooklyn was working out there, and on the staff as one of the coaches was Olson. He was telling everyone that he made a hitter out of me. "That was my boy at Pocatello," he bragged. I didn't say anything – I let him take a bow. Actually, I learned everything there myself; I learned in spite of Ivy the Terrible.

The next time I saw him was at Howard Buick down on Figueroa in Los Angeles. I was getting my car serviced, and he was the service manager. I think he stayed there a long time.

The last time I saw him was at his funeral. I was surprised that so few baseball people were there, probably only half a dozen. There wasn't anyone from the Brooklyn Club; I thought they would be well-represented there for a man who played for them in both the 1916 and 1920 World Series.

One final story about Ivy Olson. Ivy played at Brooklyn, a tough town where all the wolves come out and ride you. The papers reported that Olson used to stick cotton in his ears so that he couldn't hear them. One night we were all sitting around in front of the hotel. Olson was in a good mood for a change and one of the players called out, "Say, Ivy, tell us about stuffing cotton in your ears when you was with Brooklyn. Is it true or did the reporters just make it up?" Ivy admitted that it was true. "Sure, I did that; I wasn't going to listen to those fans getting on me. Then it didn't bother me when they yelled at me. I couldn't hear them."

I believed him. He played nine years with Brooklyn, and almost anything could happen there. He had such a terrible temper. He almost caused two riots the year I was with him. Once he told a young player to spike the second baseman when he went down to second. The player tried to follow his instructions and ended up breaking his leg.

Life was slow in Pocatello in 1927. After I got settled there, I moved into a rooming house with three other fellows. There were four young women rooming there, too. We would get together and make a lot of noise, which bothered the landlady. We paid five dollars a week for our room.

We ate our meals at a local restaurant, where the proprietor was a baseball fan, and we got a discount. You could get dinner for seventy-five cents and there were no tips. Nobody tipped in small towns in those days. We were able to save money, maybe a hundred dollars or so.

Most of us were young, twenty or twenty-one, and most of us were trying to move up in professional baseball. There were a few players who were called "baseball bums." They weren't going anywhere, but they would try to play somewhere every summer instead of working. They would jump from one league to another.

There wasn't much to do when we weren't playing. You just hung around with the fellows in the hotel lobby, or we would rent a car and drive out to a public swimming pool. Whether you could dance or not, you went to the Saturday night dance. All the farm girls would come into town and that's where we would wind up. Occasionally, a fan would invite you home for dinner, or sometimes for a bottle of home brew.

Things were quiet at the ball park, too. We drew four or five hundred people at best during the week, maybe a thousand on Sunday. About the middle of July we were ready to fold up. We were out there selling tickets, trying to bring people into the stands to keep the league going.

Pocatello led the league the second half with 31 wins and 21 losses. Idaho Falls won the first half, but dropped to last place in the second half. However, they beat us in the playoffs (four games to three) to win the League championship. If there had been no divided schedule, Ogden would have won the pennant because they had the best won/lost record for the entire season.

At the end of the season in Pocatello, Los Angeles wanted to buy me, but only after they had a look. Imagine, I led the league with .385 and hit twenty-four home runs for a league record. You can never go by the reports in the papers as to what the deal was. I was told that they bought me for $750.

I went to Los Angeles in September and they played me right away. They threw me right into the sun field – right field – where the sun in L. A. hangs low right in your eyes. I got by without getting hurt for those last two weeks. I hit .365 and a couple of home runs. They decided to keep me.

Apprenticeship

"Dirt would blow all over the place. The grounds keeper would have to get out his hose during the game and wet down the field in order to control the dust."

FOUR

JOURNEYMAN

A. The Pacific Coast League in the Twenties

Bill Schroeder, famous director of the Helms Athletic Foundation, at the time of this writing, The Citizens' Savings Athletic Foundation, is a contemporary of Wally Berger and frequently saw him play with the Angels in 1927-29.

Coincidentally, Bill played with the Hollywood High baseball team which won the Los Angeles City championship in 1922, the same year that Wally played with Mission High when they won the San Francisco City championship.

Bill was an observer of the Los Angeles baseball scene as far back as 1915, and followed the Pacific Coast League intensively. In his foundation work, he researched the PCL back to 1903, the year it was founded. After narrowing down his choices for player of the year to four or five for each of the years, he submitted the names to a committee of baseball writers: Bob Ray, *Los Angeles Times,* Johnnie Old, *Herald-Express,* Bob Hunter, *Examiner* and others. Wally was their choice as "Angel Player of the Year" for 1929.

Unquestionably, Bill Schroeder is the outstanding sports authority in the West and ranks with any in the nation. His eyewitness report is the best kind of original source material. The following three paragraphs are from an interview with him:

"Baseball was a truly wonderful game in Los Angeles in 1929. The players performed so well that it was most enjoyable. I was an avid fan. Both the Hollywood Stars and the Angels played at Wrigley Field, a major-league baseball park. Other parks in the league were not so pretentious, but they were adequate. And the interest of the fans was, I thought, exceptional.

"Since there was no major league baseball west of Cincinnati or Chicago, we had our famous Pacific Coast League, which was thriving then because times were good throughout the United States and on the West Coast. The level of play here was exceptional, too. Some of the teams, two or three of them, could have played well in the major leagues. Many of the players were of major-league caliber. Some were just climbing the ladder. Others had been in the majors and had come down and were still outstanding players.

"Wally played with the Angels in '27, '28 and '29, and he had fine seasons in all those years. He was a big fellow who was always in good condition. He was a hard batsman and a long ball hitter. He was fast, as well, and could run the bases, and was a fine outfielder with a good arm. He did everything right. In 1929 it was apparent that he was ready for the major leagues. He had all the qualifications."

The Golden Twenties, as this period in American history is often called, were lush years for baseball on the Pacific Coast. As Bill Schroeder reminds us, the American and National League teams traveled only as far west as Chicago and Cincinnati. Expansion to the West came with the development of air transportation, and with burgeoning populations in the urban centers which could support major-league franchises – this didn't happen until well after World War II. When Wally played for the Angels, the Pacific Coast League represented the best baseball available.

A favorable climate and lack of major-league competition made possible a 200-game schedule. Television was non-existent except in science fiction comics, and radio was just beginning. In fact, *Baseball Magazine* in the mid-thirties was still debating whether games should be broadcast at all!

According to the *Spalding Guide* for 1930, "The league (in 1929) drew 1,924,196 spectators. This was not the best attendance in the history of the league, but it was very good." Some of the best and most colorful players in baseball came from the PCL. In 1929 names like Jigger Statz, Elias C. Funk, Buzz Arlett, Slug Tolson, Duster Mails, Truck Hannah and Zip Dumovich sprinkled the sports pages of the metropolitan papers. Future great players Lefty Gomez, Ernie Lombardi, Frank Crosetti and Adolph Camilli (along with Wally) went to the majors from the Pacific Coast League.

With two hundred or more games played per season, statistics in the PCL seemed incredible in comparison with other leagues. Ike Boone of the San Francisco Missions was the league batting champion in 1929 with a batting average of .407 in 198 games. He was at bat 794 times and had 323 hits, including 55 home runs and 29 two-baggers. He scored 195 runs and batted in 218.

Wally, who was at bat 744 times in 199 games, had more modest--but nevertheless very impressive--statistics. He had 249 hits, including 40 home runs and 41 two-base hits. He scored 170 runs and batted in 166.

Ike Boone went up again to Brooklyn, but he played in only 40 games, batting .297, scoring 13 runs and batting in 13. Wally, of course, went up to the Boston Braves and had a sensational first year. Gomez went to the Yankees, winning 2 and losing 5. The next year, however, he won 21 and lost 9 – staying up for 14 years. Lombardi did not make it until 1931, but lasted 17 years. Crosetti made it with the Yankees and was a great shortstop until after World War II. Camilli went to the Chicago Cubs three years later.

B. Making It with the Angels

Early in February, 1928, I drove down from San Francisco to Los Angeles for spring training with the Angels. They held spring training right in their own ball park, Wrigley Field. I was surprised at the weather for February; sometimes it was pretty warm, and often there were really hot days. So we got out to the ball park and began to get into condition.

Pay for the season didn't begin until the league opened in April. They gave us living expenses and we lived right in town. It wasn't much, but it was adequate – probably about $4 per day. I was single then. I got a room near the ball park for $6 a week and would eat in a drug store right near the park. Breakfast cost 25 to 30 cents. I could eat all day for a couple of dollars. From where I lived, I could walk to Wrigley Field. I saved money on transportation.

We started training slowly. We'd get to the park at about 10:00 a.m., lap the park a few times, then get on the side and play catch for a little while. Then we might get into a pepper game and fool around like that. We might not have batting practice for the first two or three days. We had to give the pitchers a chance to loosen up their arms. Near the end of the first week, we would divide into squads for batting practice.

We had two workouts a day. Batting practice was followed by infield practice. Outfielders would shag fly balls. We'd finish the first workout with a few laps around the field, then quit around noon and take time out for a box lunch. We didn't leave the park and we didn't go to a restaurant. We didn't change anything but our sweatshirts and maybe the jockstrap.

After lunch we would play an inter-squad game for three or four innings. The gates were open for these workouts. There was quite a crowd there. Workouts were free to the public, and sometimes as many as 400-500 people would drop in to watch and get acquainted with the newer players. After about two weeks, we started playing serious baseball.

Our parent organization, the Chicago Cubs, trained at Catalina Island. They advertised Catalina for Mr. Wrigley by having spring training there. In the newsreels at the movies, one learned about the glories of Catalina. Actually, it wasn't too good a place to train, because of the cool wind which most players didn't like. After a couple of weeks, the Cubs would come over to the mainland and take over Wrigley Field, and we started playing them a game every day. Of course, Monday was always an off day.

During the regular season in the Pacific Coast League, we would play every day except Monday. There was a double-header every Sunday. Monday was our day off, but frequently it was a travel day. We played a seven-game schedule with each team and we'd meet each team four times, which would be approximately 196 games. In 1928 the Angels played 191 games. I played in only 138 of them, as I missed the last six weeks. In 1929, the Angels played 202 games, of which I played 199.

We used to argue as to which of the leagues was best among the minor leagues. Ball players from other minor leagues, like the American Association or the International League, would like to come to the Pacific Coast League because they liked the weather and they got an extra month's pay because of our longer season.

On a typical day at home, we were free to do what we wanted after we finished playing. Usually the young fellows would hang around together. The veteran players – most of whom were married and lived in apartments nearby – went on their way. We didn't know what they did and no one knew what we did. In the neighborhood, we got to meet girls. We would date them and go to the movies or down to Venice Beach to ride the roller coaster. Sometimes we played cards or were invited to people's houses. Most of the time it was poker – it was the most popular game with the players then.

Most of us had baseball on our minds first. At least I thought about my career all the time. I got to the ball park early. I was one of those guys who'd be there when the trainer showed up. On a warm day it was nice to strip off all your clothes and run around the club house in a jockstrap. If I had aches or pains, it was a good time to have them worked on.

We would go through a light workout before the game – loosen up, have batting practice, pepper games and shag flies. The minor-league managers didn't have coaches. They ran the whole show themselves. He'd appoint an old-timer to help him out. He designated who was going to hit to the infield and who hit to the outfield. He made out the lineup. Then when the game got underway, he coached at first base. (Even today, I don't think that minor-league managers have the luxury of coaches to assist them. The manager probably still drives the bus for some teams!)

When we went on the road to play, we would be in each town for a week. We would unpack our bags, hang up our clothes and settle in. Then we'd move on to the next town. We traveled exclusively by train; there was no air transportation then. Due to slow transportation, there were no major-league teams in the West – they couldn't schedule it right. In those days, it took three days to get from Los Angeles or San Francisco to Chicago. Seattle and Portland were our long trips north, but they always tied the two cities together on our schedule.

We had our own Pullman car. The regular players who played every day slept in the lower berths. The pitchers usually slept in the uppers – except the one who was scheduled to pitch the next day. The porter would leave the middle bunks down and put up the end ones so that we could sit and play cards. If it was a long trip, there would be a dining car on the train and the food was good. However, the trains weren't air-conditioned then. In July and August it was terribly hot as we went through places like Red Bluff and Redding. We just sat in our car, streaming with perspiration.

Going to Seattle, we'd spend our day off traveling in order to get there for Tuesday's game. One time the train was late and Seattle kept working out, waiting for us to show. We put on our uniforms, warmed up a little and started the game. We had been on the train a couple of days, all bound up. We didn't have any practice at all – no batting practice, infield practice, nothing. And we beat them!

In Sacramento on a Sunday it was called a double-header, but it was really two games. We would get up early in the morning, go to the Sacramento Park, put on our uniforms, and take a bus to Stockton. At 10:00 a.m. there we would play the morning game. You would think people wouldn't be out there, but the Stockton crowd was waiting. They had one of those rough-looking ball parks with a rough diamond.

Today there would be a lot of grumbling about something like that, but we had to take it in stride. Then we hopped back into the bus and rode in all that heat and humidity back to Sacramento. They gave us a box lunch. Then we changed our uniforms and played the afternoon game in Sacramento. Two separate crowds – two separate admissions – you had to be young to do what we did!

On Sundays in San Francisco we played a morning game and an afternoon game. The park was very small – about 13,000 capacity. The mornings were nice and calm, but you could dispense with the afternoons. The wind would come down from Twin Peaks and blow in that ball park so hard that you couldn't hit one out of there. Dirt would blow all over the place. The grounds keeper would have to get out his hose during the game and wet down the field in order to control the dust. In Oakland, we also played morning and afternoon games, but never in Los Angeles. We played the double-header in the afternoon.

We didn't have to travel to play Hollywood. They used our park, Wrigley Field, for their home ground. When they were the home team at our park, they would come to bat last, and we'd have to wear our road uniforms. We would get mad and say, "They're trying to run us out of our own ball park."

We had a good rivalry there. It was as if we were two separate towns – they had their fans and we had ours. If we had a good series, we would fill the park on a Sunday for a double-header; Wrigley Field held 18,000. On a Saturday game with Hollywood or San Francisco, we might draw 10,000. On a weekday, 1200-2000 would be a fair crowd.

A Triple-A club in those days consisted mainly of veterans who had been in the big leagues. When you joined them, you were supposed to know how to play. In 1928, the Angels had all veteran players except Wes Schulmerich and me. The manager was not a teacher, and the players chewed you out if you made the wrong play. They didn't hold back: "What the hell are you trying to do, you knucklehead?" They told you what you should have done. You learned that way or you asked questions. Freddie Haney taught me a great deal by criticizing me when I did something wrong, then explaining the reasons to me.

The only time I ever remember getting any specific instruction was when Marty Krug, the manager of the Angels, taught me base-running and base-stealing. He had a special interest in this aspect of the game, so he took the time to help me. If I got picked

**WALLY SLAMS A HOMER
AND WINS A NEW $100 SUIT!**

off or made some mistake, he would tell me right there, and show me what to do, and I'd follow him.

I was fast and I got to be a good base-runner. I enjoyed running the bases. I'd go for an extra base and not get thrown out when there was a better than fifty-fifty chance to make it. I got to know when to run, when to go and when not to go. Marty Krug had been a great base-runner and stealer himself, and he was a good teacher. I think of him when I watch games on television and see all those mistakes on the bases.

By the way, there was no formal instruction in the major leagues, either. We had two coaches there, one for first base and the other to pitch batting practice. In Boston, at least, their job seemed primarily to attend banquets and service clubs. They were out there speaking all the time.

The manager in the Coast League was no baby-sitter, either. There weren't any rules about getting in at night or getting up for breakfast or things like that. It was best to get up early enough to have a good breakfast. You had to be at the ball park by noon. It was just taken for granted that you'd be in bed by midnight. They didn't have anyone watching you. You were on your honor. Generally the young guys were careful. They wanted to get ahead and so they kept their noses clean.

Marty Krug didn't want a lot of young players – he wanted veterans. In a sense, he was saying, "Here you are, let's play the game. You all know what to do." It was good for me, because I learned from observation and from asking questions.

You can see what the job was like. You had to work hard at it. Naturally, some of the old-timers who had come down didn't. They knew that this was the end of the road. I heard one say, "After this season in the Coast League or the Southern League, I'm through; I can't take it anymore."

C. Paternalistic Mr. Patrick

One thing I discovered in my first year with the Angels was that a player who got sick or hurt, particularly if the player was a good prospect, was treated with consideration. Quite a difference from what happened to me in Pocatello with my bad leg.

Near the end of my first year with Los Angeles, I got this fever; at first I didn't know what it was. I was having trouble breathing and I was very hot. I asked the other players in the dugout if it was hot and sticky: "Yeah, Wally, it's pretty close." I played with that fever for a couple of days and let myself get run down. I sweated like hell, losing twenty pounds. I found a doctor in the phone book, and he told me to stay in bed.

The people at the house on Manchester Boulevard where I was staying asked me about it and I told them about the doctor I called. They said immediately, "Oh, no, not him! We'll get you our family doctor." *He* said that I had intestinal flu, a touch of pneumonia and the start of peritonitis – because I had played with a fever. He gave me medicine and I stayed in bed a week.

When I went back to the club, I told them that I was very weak and had lost a lot of weight. Up to that point I had had a good season. I was used to the league and was batting .327 in 138 games. Mr. Patrick, President of the Angels and a business associate of Mr. Wrigley, listened sympathetically. He said, "Go over to Catalina and get yourself well. Just show this card. It's good for everything. You can go home anytime you want."

It was a free ride for everything. I showed the card to the men on the boat – no charge. At the hotel and restaurant it was good for everything – didn't cost me a penny, and I got my regular pay for the rest of the season, too.

After about three days in Catalina, I got a little lonesome. It was after Labor Day and there weren't many vacationers left on the island. I hopped the boat back to the mainland and went home to San Francisco. I ate like a horse, drank milk shakes and eggs, but I could hardly gain any weight. Finally I started to pick up a little bit. I got back to normal and started the 1929 season on time.

During the '29 season I injured my knee sliding into third base. I slid too close, hitting straight into the bag, jamming my knee, which promptly swelled up. They sent me to a doctor at 7th and Grand in downtown Los Angeles, who examined it and told me that "a little fluid got under there." He worked off the fluid by manipulation and by exercising the knee. "I think I got it all out; you can go ahead and play." I want to Marty Krug and told him the doctor said I could play. I wanted to play because I was doing very well.

To my surprise, Marty said, "To hell with the doctor. I want you to take three or four days off and make sure that it's all right." After all, I was a prospect and they didn't want me to risk further injury.

Mr. J. H. Patrick, President of the Angels, deserves further mention. He was very good to me. I've mentioned his generosity when I was recovering from the flu. That was only one of a number of times he was kind or helpful. The first time was really important to me. I had a bad day in right field. I lost the ball in the sun and got hit on the top of my head. The fans got on me and razzed me. I just tipped my hat to them and jogged off the field at the end of the inning. The headline next day in the *Examiner* over Martin Burke's column read: **BERGER CATCHES ONE FLY – ON HIS FOREHEAD.** In his story, he made me seem ridiculous.

That bad day in right field made me downcast. I wanted very badly to make the club and I thought the incident was going to put me back. The very next day, as I came into the park, Mr. Patrick called me over to talk with him; he knew I was feeling bad. He said to me, "I like the way you took it out there when you tipped your hat. Right field is a tough position in this park – the sun is bad. We're (he meant himself and the manager) going to play you in left field. The job is yours. You've got it all year, so don't worry." I never forgot the gesture. It built up my confidence at a time when I needed it – and I went on and played well for the rest of the season until I got sick.

Mr. Patrick was a kind of patron of the art of baseball. He was a dedicated baseball fan. He loved the game, and when a player performed well in some way, he liked to show that he was pleased. For instance, he wanted the Angel players to look good on and off the field, so he would give them suits of clothes as a special reward. He had a box seat right near the Angel dugout. One day I hit a long home run; as I returned to the dugout, he called me over and told me to get myself a suit of clothes.

From "Notes on the Angels" in the *Los Angeles Examiner:* "Charley Tolson won't need a new suit of clothes for a long time. Both he and Walter Berger received orders for suits from Prexy Joe Patrick for smacking out homers in the third."

I thanked him and told the boys in the dugout what he had said. They told me where the store was located downtown. The following week I went down to 8th and Hill to get myself the suit. I asked the tailor about the price. He said, "We start at $100 and up." Not wanting to be greedy, I asked for something in the $100 range. He showed me the various kinds of material available and I had one made to order. Later in the season, Mr. Patrick told me to get another. I was beginning to get a good wardrobe. I'd never paid more than $30 for a suit, myself.

Even after I was no longer with the Angels – when I was with the Braves – he saw me at a Chicago game. He waved me over to his box for a friendly chat. I felt honored – a poor boy from the Mission District of San Francisco – talking casually with a multi-millionaire.

In my second year with the Angels I was hitting the ball hard, and I became established in left field, being second in the league to Jigger Statz in putouts. I would have caught more and Jigger less if he hadn't covered so much territory. He didn't leave much room for me and the right-fielder. Jigger had 517 putouts in 195 games in center field, while I had 449 in 193 games in left field.

As the season wore on, the rumors about my being sold appeared more and more. One week I was going to the Pirates, the next week the Philadelphia Athletics and Connie Mack were making inquiries. Most often it was the Cubs who were going to take me, naturally, since we were all the property of the Cubs. Finally, it appeared as if I was going to be held at Los Angeles for a third year.

The headlines in the Los Angeles sports pages announced that Mr. Wrigley wanted me for the Cubs and that he had "ordered the Los Angeles Club to hold on to Berger for another season. Wrigley thinks that, by 1931, the youngster will be able to crash into the Cubs' lineup." They also reported that "The Athletics, Giants, Braves and the Indians put in bids for Berger." It was also stated that the Angels manager wanted to keep Berger back for an additional year.

What the manager probably had in mind was keeping me back with Wes Schulmerich. Jigger Statz was playing center. We had a good-hitting team in 1929, but the pitching staff was weak. The pitchers gave up more runs than we drove in. The manager was trying to keep the team intact and strengthen his pitching staff. It turned out that the Cubs' management had different ideas.

My feeling was that I had put in two years and I wanted to get going. I wanted to hit that big league before I got too old. To get to the big leagues is tough – I figured that if you don't make the jump after four years in the minors, if you don't develop it in four years, you shouldn't fool with baseball.

The life of a baseball player is just so long, and I was putting on age. I used to sit around with the players and talk about how they trade you or sell you and you have nothing to say about it. You can't pick your town. You can't say, "I don't want to go to New York!" They tell you that you're going to go or you don't play. I was thinking about that when they finally sold me – and I tried to get a piece of the purchase price they got for me.

WALLY'S FIRST ATTEMPT AT BARGAINING —
GETS $1 RAISE

FIVE

THE BOTTOM LINE

A. Negotiations with Moise & Klinker, Butte and Pocatello

When I was in high school, I worked at Moise and Klinker in downtown San Francisco. They sold office supplies and had a print shop. I was getting five dollars a week working after school. They taught me how to run their printing press – hand feed it. Pretty soon, I was running all their advertisements and other office printing right off that machine.

I decided that if I'm going to handle that printing press, I'm going down and ask old Moise for a raise. I can see him now, with one of those VanDyke beards. When I asked him for more money, he paused and said to me, "Let's see, now, how long have you been with us?" I told him and explained, "I'm running that printing press now, and I think I ought to get a raise."

He thought it over and finally said, "I'll give you six dollars a week." That was the result of my first attempt to bargain. A dollar more a week doesn't sound like much now, but it would buy quite a bit in 1922, and it was a twenty per cent raise.

Not long after that, the place burned down, gutted by fire. They wanted to keep me on to clean up, but I refused. I wanted to play ball. I'd received a wire from the manager of the Anaconda Copper Mining Team. He wanted to know how much I wanted to come up there and play at Butte. I said, "$275 a month and transportation both ways." They accepted the terms and gave me the transportation.

See, when I left home to play ball in Montana, I had round-trip transportation. All the boys in the pool hall agreed, "If you sign a contract, Wally, make sure you get a round-trip ticket so you have a way of gettin' back. You don't want to be stuck a thousand miles away. Get your transportation both ways. They may cut you loose. Be sure you can get home."

Hanging around playgrounds and playing semi-pro, there's always a fellow or two here and there who's played some minor league ball, and they tell you these things. They probably got cut loose back there in Binghamton, New York – or someplace else – and had to find their way across the country. That's why they teach you these things – the fellows themselves.

And so you learn from the street, right? No coaching. My father didn't know anything about it. Nobody but those guys who had been around knew anything, and they'd tell you.

There were lots of guys looking for jobs in professional ball those days. They were semi-pro players, or they played "D" League ball, and they'd get in a car and tour all those minor leagues and work out at trying to get a job.

I remember four guys doing that. They went down to the Mississippi Valley League and the Three-I League. They toured there and they would go to a town where these teams were working out and they'd ask the manager for a try-out.

Sometimes one got signed up and then the other three would go on to another place and try to get hooked up. Well, they were trying to get jobs. I know there were a lot of minor leagues then, quite a few "D" League teams around the country, and that's a place to start. No money in it, but if you like to play – $200 a month. You couldn't go very far on that.

So I'm playing in Butte, I think for $275, when they asked me by wire how much I wanted to come down to Pocatello. I said, "I'll take $275 a month." They wired back that they had a salary limit: "We'll give you $200." I wired back, "I'll take it." I only had playing every day on my mind. Money wasn't important to me then.

I was thinking about a career. I wasn't thinking about the money, as long as they gave me enough to eat. So then I told the manager in Butte after I agreed by wire – which is a contract – I knew that, even when I was a kid. I went up to the manager's house, knocked on the door and his wife answered. "He's shaving, he'll be right with you." He came out and said, "What's on your mind?" I answered, "I have a chance to go to Pocatello and play every day and play in the outfield."

I thought it'd be all right and he'd say, "Go ahead." Instead, he said, "Wait a minute, we were gonna put you back on short. We were gonna try you in the outfield. I don't want you to leave. Besides, we paid your transportation up here."

I said, "I'm sorry, but I already agreed down there in Pocatello." They couldn't do nothing about it because I was independent. It wasn't organized ball. Then I said, "Tell you what

I'll do...I've worked for three weeks and I got pay coming. You take my transportation out of the money you owe me." Finally I asked him: "I owe room and board. Will you take it and pay this family the money I owe them, too?"

B. Berger as Bargainer

When Walter Berger turned down Judge Fuchs' offer at the end of his first year with the Braves and became a holdout, it was apparent that the Judge was not dealing with a naive youth from small-town America. Wally was a man twenty-five years old who had supported himself for a decade in various jobs in San Francisco, a cosmopolitan center with a reputation for being a "labor town."

Moreover, Wally had lived in a baseball environment since his junior high school days, hanging around Seals Park and Kenealy's Pool Hall. Also, he had developed, tested and sharpened his baseball skills for eight years – five years of semi-pro ball in San Francisco and three years in the minor leagues, the last two years with the Angels in the Pacific Coast League.

Berger's character was shaped in the home of hard-working German immigrant parents, and in the rough-and-tumble of the Mission District of San Francisco. As soon as he was able to earn money, he was expected to help support the family. He was taught to be quiet and respectful of his elders, but also to stand up for himself.

By the time Wally entered high school, he was independent and resourceful. This is clearly revealed in his account of his bargaining with the firm of Moise and Klinker. It is a scene which reminds one of both Charles Dickens and Horatio Alger, Jr.

In the Twenties and Thirties, bargaining was individual, not collective. There was no Players' Association. No skilled negotiators, like the player's representative or agent of today, spoke for the player. It was every man for himself.

The player got the best advice he could from the old-timers of his acquaintance. Wally received his guidance from the veteran Fred Haney, one of the wisest of the tribe, but he was on his own to deal with management. It was usually a very uneven contest.

The Baseball Establishment drafted the Uniform Players' Contract. It made all the rules, interpreted the rules and enforced the rules. Its behavior was paternalistic, arbitrary and unilateral.

71

Even if the player held out and signed a contract at a satisfactory figure, he could be released any day of the season and was entitled to only ten days' pay. This happened to Wally in his last year at Cincinnati.

Of course, the situation of the ball player as an employee was not unique in this regard. Most workers in the Twenties and Thirties were in the same boat. Any day – but usually on Friday – an employee might find a pink slip in his pay envelope, notifying him that "his services were no longer required."

During his first three years in organized baseball, Wally shrewdly established himself as a professional performer. Salary was not his primary concern. He accepted the contracts offered to him and kept his eye on the ball. His first real confrontation with management came when he learned of his sale to the Boston Braves by the Los Angeles Angels for a reported $40,000 to $50,000.

Wally went promptly and boldly to the office of Boots Weber, the club secretary, and asked for a cut of the purchase price. Five thousand dollars, he thought, was a fair share. Weber brushed him off by reminding him that he was now "the property of the Boston Braves," and would have to deal with them.

It was an impossible situation for a first-year man. Wally accepted it philosophically, biding his time. But from that point on in his playing career, he always asserted himself firmly and respectfully in the attempt to get an appropriate salary for services performed.

Wally, as the reader will see, proved to be a very courageous and tough-minded bargainer. The letters and documents make it possible for the reader to share – to an unusual degree – Wally's experience.

C. Advice from the Toughest Old-Timer of All

Old-timers had a saying: "Once a cheap ball player, always a cheap ball player." They said it because from experience they knew that once you sign a contract low, it's going to be tough to get it back up. You got your advice from older players who'd been through the mill.

We didn't have agents or lawyers. Just from listening to them you thought about negotiating their way. Ball players knew from their experience that once you become known as a cheap ball player, you'll always be one.

When you were asking for an amount of money, they said to go high and up. It's easy to come down and tough to go up. So you ask for more and then maybe when you're coming down, you get about what you wanted. You don't take their first offer. This is advice from an old-timer. "Don't take their first offer, *never!*" Hold out if you only get $50.00 a month more. Hold out just on the general principle that they're getting you cheap." (Quoting Edd Roush, the great outfielder, who was always holding out – with the Cincinnati Reds and the New York Giants, 1916-1931.)

Ball players in the old days had to negotiate for themselves. Players who were all getting different rates didn't discuss what they were getting. It was just an accepted practice that you didn't ask the other guy how much a year he was making. We never told them and they never asked us. It would have been a breach of etiquette or whatever you want to call it.

That policy of silence worked for management, of course, but you didn't want to tell the other guy what you were making. You may have been making more than he was and he's thinking, "I'm as good as him; why ain't I getting that money?" So to keep any friction away from the ball club, you just kept your mouth shut and let 'em guess.

The newspaper guys guess. They put out a list of salaries which clubs are paying and when it comes down to your name, you know they're way off. You're not getting as much as they put down. You say, "I'm probably worth that, but I know what I'm getting and they're guessing."

A good example of what I mean about being a cheap ball player was a young pitcher with the Braves. One day I asked, "When's your wife coming up to Boston?" Here it was June, and everybody else's wife was there. He said, "I can't afford it. They are paying me only $450 a month." And rent in Boston was at least $100 a month. He said that he just had to leave her home. Remember that he got paid only for the months he was playing – he had to do something else in the off-season.

As we discussed it, he explained that he didn't expect to make the big-league club. He figured he just come to spring training and spring back to one of their farm clubs. He did pretty well in spring training, so they put him on the parent club roster, but they didn't raise his contract.

If they were going to put him on the roster, they should have torn up his old contract and given him a decent salary. If I had been the ball player, I'd have made them give me a new contract. He did turn out to be one of the starting pitchers. He was no star or anything like that, but he impressed the manager and was kept on.

As I was saying, they got him as cheap as they could. He was a farm boy from out there in the country and $450 a month looked pretty big during the depression. They probably told him: "Now you're in the big leagues and if you have a good year, we'll take care of you." Which, of course, meant nothing; you have to get it down in black and white.

But, again, you played only six months – that's only what – $2,700? And you weren't able to save a lot. Your expenses in the big cities in the East were up there. This was in the mid-Thirties. I was paying $45 a month for a furnished apartment in Los Angeles, but you couldn't get anything in Boston for less than $65 – and that wasn't good. In this case, the player made a living in baseball for another ten years. Nothing spectacular, but he survived until he was thirty-seven.

Another bit of advice which I got from the old-timers was never to borrow from the club. Some ball payers couldn't save a dime and they'd always wind up broke. Then they would write the ball club or call them up and ask them to send money on next year's contract. Now they were into the club for money. That was bad, because once you borrow from them, you're stuck. You can't argue your contract with them. You're not in any position to negotiate.

Even if you were, it was tough for the average player to bargain for himself. He was usually outmatched. Take the case of Wattie Holm, who tried to bargain with perhaps the toughest and shrewdest of them all. Wattie told me about his attempt to get more money when he was playing with the Cardinals. He decided to challenge the great Branch Rickey, "The Mahatma." Everybody knew that the St. Louis Cardinals was a cheap organization. The pay was low and Wattie was mad enough about the offer to face up to Rickey.

Wattie said, "I was gonna go in there and tell him I wanted so much more for the season and I wasn't gonna budge. I walked into the outer office with fire in my eye and announced myself." Rickey said, "Wattie, come on in. Have a seat and I'll be with you in a minute."

"So I sat down and waited. Rickey is sitting there with

papers and forms all over his desk. He's talking to Houston, telling them to move this player over to Danville. He takes this guy here and puts him over there. He sends somebody to Rochester and moves somebody from Rochester. He's moving players all around the country.

"He's keeping all these conversations going and remembering the names of all these ball players here and there. The way he was talking I could see right away that he was going to out-talk me. I knew I wasn't going to get first base with him."

"Finally, after sitting there a little while longer, I said, 'Hand me the contract – I'll sign the damn thing.' I gave up. I signed the contract; the hell with it."

D. Berger Becomes Property

In his first year in organized baseball (1927) with Pocatello of the Utah-Idaho League, Wally led the league in home runs and batting average. He also made more put-outs than any other outfielder.

Pocatello sold Wally for $750, "just for a look," to Los Angeles. The Angels looked at him for the last fourteen games of the season and liked what they saw. He batted .365 and hit three home runs.

After two good seasons with the Angels, he became "the property of the Boston Braves" who purchased him "for an unannounced sum" (reportedly between $40,000 and $50,000). Reading about the sale price in the newspaper, Wally had the audacity to ask the Angels for a cut of the price they had received for him.

When the Angels bought me from Pocatello, I didn't even bargain with them. I loved the game and I wanted a career in baseball. They sent me a contract for $350 a month for six months. I just signed it and sent it back. I didn't argue; I was happy with it. I was playing in fast company and had a chance to go to the big leagues.

Then I had a pretty good season in 1928, so they raised me to $500. Anyway, when I read in the paper that they sold me to Boston for forty or fifty thousand, I thought how cheap they had got me from Pocatello. I decided to ask for a cut of the purchase price.

So I went down to the Angels' office in Wrigley Tower at 41st and Avalon. I was hoping to get a $5,000 piece. After all, I didn't make much money in the minor leagues. I thought I'd get a little bit now. I'd just got married and I wanted a little bit of cushion there.

I went to Boots Weber, the club secretary, and said, "You know, Mr. Weber, I should get a piece of the purchase price. I should get something out of you. You sell me for forty or fifty thousand and I didn't cost you a dime."

He said, "No, Wally, you'll have to argue with Boston. They own you now. Besides, the Angel organization and the Chicago Cubs' organization won't go for something like that. It's out of our hands. You are now the property of the Boston Braves. You'll have to deal with them."

Boston sent my first contract in the spring of 1930 or earlier. It was for $4,500. I held out immediately and they told me that I was a bit green on negotiating. They said, "After all, you're only a rookie. You've got to come up and prove that you're a big-league ball player. And we're giving you the standard increase over your minor league salary. You come up and show us what you can do and then we'll talk about what you can get the second year."

I finally agreed. I could see that I wasn't going to get anywhere. I didn't have anything to fight with. They said I'd have to prove myself, so with that thought in mind, I went to spring training.

WALLY, 1930, ROOKIE OF THE YEAR
WITH 38 HOME RUNS — A RECORD!

SIX

FROM FUCHS TO QUINN TO BERGER

A. Fred Haney, Financial Counselor (1931)

In 1930, his first year with the Boston Braves, Wally Berger hit 38 home runs, a record for a rookie, which lasted until 1987 when Mark McGwire of Oakland broke his record by hitting 49 home runs. Wally still holds the record in the National League.

Wally's batting average was .310, and his slugging average was .614 (a .500 slugging average is very good). His SA was so high because forty-six per cent of his hits were for extra bases. His importance to the Boston offense was very apparent. He drove in fifty-eight more runs than any other Boston hitter, and the rest of the Boston squad hit only twenty-eight home runs.

In the letter which contained my contract for 1931, Judge Fuchs wrote: "Enclosed please find a contract for $7,000, which is an increase of $3,000 over last year's contract. I went over the situation with Manager McKechnie and we both appreciate that you, for a first-year man, made a creditable showing. I am personally adding an extra $500, which I do not desire to have appear in the contract, but upon the signing of same by you we shall mail you a check for $500, which is my method of giving you an extra reward for your diligent, faithful service and as a medium of encouragement to you."

When my contract arrived, I went to Fred Haney for help. Freddie had given me good advice when we played together for the Angels. That winter I was playing for him in the winter league in Los Angeles. He managed the Kelley Kars team in a pretty fast league made up mostly of professionals and some good college boys. Kelley was a car dealer who sponsored us and furnished the uniforms. We played every Sunday at Wrigley Field, the home of the Angels. I knew Fred had negotiated with Branch Rickey, the

79

smartest guy in baseball, and held his own. So I asked Freddie, "What do you think I ought to get?"

He answered quickly, "You ought to get more than $7,000. You had a very good year. Don't be a cheap ball player. Once you sign for that, you're going to be a cheap ball player all the rest of your time up there. Get all you can while you're able to. Let's ask them for $12,000."

"Freddie," I said, "they won't pay me no $12,000."

Haney replied, "Let's ask." And we did.

What Fred predicted would happen came true. The letters came and the telegrams followed. They were getting anxious for me to get to spring training. That's when they wrote that "You are being ill-advised." That's great.

Today you get all kinds of advice and you don't even have to ask for the money. Everyone else is doing the talking. Well, we hustled around; Fred advised me whenever he could. Finally, they came up to $10,000. It was getting close to spring training, so I said, "Fred, I'm going to sign up. I want to get to spring training."

He replied, "You can get a couple thousand more. Just hang on. They'll want you there." But I responded, "Fred, I think I'll settle for the $10,000. I want to get going. I want to have another good year and get more money on top of that."

Maybe I should have taken his advice and held out for more. I think they got me cheap and were happy I signed. That was in February, 1931. Wes Schulmerich and I made the transcontinental journey in his coupe in six-and-a-half days. We arrived in St. Petersburg on February 22.

B. Sophomore Year (1932); A Small Increase

In his sophomore season in the National League (1931), Wally had another good year. Despite the "dead" ball which had been adopted that year, he placed third in home runs behind Chuck Klein (who was hitting in the "bandbox" in Philadelphia known as Baker Bowl), and Mel Ott at the Polo Grounds in New York – where the annual home run production was more than double that at Wally's home park in Boston.

Wally was second in the League in two-base hits, with 44. In total bases, he was fourth with 316. His slugging percentage was .512, and his batting average was .323, which was thirteen points better than his previous year – although the sacrifice fly rule had been eliminated.

Among outfielders in both the National and American Leagues, he was second only to Lloyd Waner, who had 484 put-outs and 20 assists. Wally had 457 put-outs and 16 assists.

By contrast, the leading outfielder in the American League, Tom Oliver of the Boston Red Sox, had 433 put-outs and 15 assists.

In their second year in the majors, many players do not do as well as they did their first. After all, if you're a pitcher, for example, the batters know you better and have had a year to study you. If you're a hitter, the pitchers have learned how to throw to you. So it's not surprising that a player slips a little – or maybe a lot. They call it the "sophomore jinx."

It didn't happen to me. I had a good year, even though I didn't hit as many home runs. Early in the season, I connected with the "deadened" ball (with the raised seams) as hard as I ever hit one; to my surprise, it was only a fly ball to deep left field. I decided then and there to hit for the average instead of trying to hit for the fence.

I found out another thing that year. No matter how well you do, or no matter how hard you try, the fans always expect you to come through every time they come to the park.

But I didn't expect that kind of thing from the experts. When I read in the *Spalding's Official Baseball Guide 1932* that "Berger had been expected to be an advanced player because he did well in 1930, but he did not improve greatly..." I was really mad. I played hard every game with a team that lost ninety games and finished in seventh place.

On January 22, 1932, Judge Fuchs, owner and President of the Boston Braves, sent me a letter containing a contract for $10,000. I held out immediately. I was supposed to report to the West Coast Inn in St. Petersburg on March 1. On February 19, I wrote a response to the Judge:

"It is only within reason for a player to expect an increase with each succesful year and the size of the increase in accordance to the value that he is to the club. In my case, the amount tendered to me is not quite sufficient. I came through with another successful year, a better year in fact than the preceding one. I feel that I drew enough people at the gate and was popular enough with the Boston fans to be worth $12,000 a year to your club."

"The Great Depression reached its lowest depth in the Winter of 1932-33. In 1933 Wall had to bargain in an almost impossibl economic and political climate."

On March 23, I still had not signed and the Judge wrote to me as follows:

"You are holding up a large number of contracts which are all signed and completed, yours being the only one outstanding...I hope and expect that our relationship will continue to be amicable and pleasant and my personal opinion is that you will do far better being guided by one who has had his players' welfare in mind...As we decided the salary offered to you for the the coming season, everything taken into consideration, is just and fair, it will not serve your best purpose to delay signing any longer."

After more exchanges in St. Petersburg, I finally settled for a small increase. However, the figures on the contract didn't really mean a thing if something happened and they wanted to get rid of you. The bottom line on the first page of the National League's Uniform Player's Contract read:

"TERMINATION (b) This contract may be terminated at any time by the Club or by any assignee upon ten days' written notice to the Player." Any day in the week they could give you your release and you got only two weeks' pay.

All the players were aware that it could happen to them. Considering the times, depression and all, they accepted it. That's the way baseball was in those days. You could be on the road and they'd hand you a release and give you two weeks' pay.

It happened all the time. You come to Boston with your family and all your belongings, and the first thing you know, you're "free." It was a good thing to have a few bucks in the bank to make sure you had the money to get back home.

The players didn't have a chance in those days. They didn't have anyone to go to bat for them. Now they have their union, and management can't do that to them.

C. Deep Depression Bargaining (1933)

The Great Depression reached its lowest depths in the Winter of 1932-33. In 1933 Wally had to bargain in an almost impossible economic and political climate.

In January, *Baseball Magazine* took up the cause of management. It expressed indignation at "greedy ballplayers," and advocated cuts of "top-heavy payrolls," citing the salaries of Ruth at $75,000, Hornsby at $40,000 and Simmons at $30,000.

In April, the editors singled out The Babe for criticism because he refused a contract of $50,000. They warned him that "his days of usefulness are rapidly nearing their close." In the same issue of the magazine, James M. Gould, in his article, "Hold-Overs, Hold-Ups and Hold-Outs," said that "major league owners were in grim earnest" in their determination to cut salaries of players. Wally, of course, was one of the culprits to whom he was referring.

Wally slipped statistically in hitting in 1932. He was number nine in home runs with 17, but this figure must be placed in perspective. The top slugger on the first-place Chicago Cubs hit 13. The leader for the second-place Pittsburgh Pirates had a total of seven. Klein and Ott were tied for first place with 38. Terry was next with 28, and Hurst of Philadelphia had twenty-four.

All four were hitting in home parks with short right-field fences, and all four were left-handers. To make the point quickly: one year at the Polo Grounds (home field for Ott and Terry), the total home run production was 150; that same year at Baker Bowl (home for Klein and Hurst), the total was 120 – but at spacious Crosley Field in Cincinnati, the total was 36. The home team hit eighteen, as did all the visiting teams together.

Wally's batting average was well-within the "magic circle" at .307. His slugging percentage dropped to .468. In 145 games, he accounted for 146 runs, scoring 90 and batting in 73. He was number nine in total bases with 282, and number eleven in total hits, with 185.

It should be noted at this point that, while Wally was always known best for his hitting prowess, the fact that he was one of the great fielders in baseball is often ignored. In 1932, he got into the record book for his fielding performance: "In fielding, Walter A. Berger, Boston, tops the outfielders with .993, which ties the record of Louis B. Duncan, Cincinnati, made in 1923." *(Spalding's Official Baseball Guide, 1933.)*

He made only three errors in 409 total chances in center field. In eleven games at first base, he had 102 put-outs, four assists, seven double plays and no errors.

The Judge sent me a long letter on January 11, 1933, trying to convince me to take a "voluntary" cut. He said that he didn't want to place "an arbitrary figure of reduction," but would leave it up to me to suggest a figure.

Since I had moved from Wilton Place in Los Angeles to Culver City, the Judge's first letter had to be forwarded to me. His second letter arrived on January 31, before I had answered his first. In it he stated the figure of $9,000, which he thought that I would have suggested if I had received his letter! Since it must be read to be appreciated, I have included the entire letter, as well as my complete response to it.

Waiting until February 10, 1933 (I wasn't in any hurry), I sent the Judge a polite refusal. I didn't mention that he was a poor mind-reader. I just told him that I would not consider a cut, but that I would sign for the same amount that I received in 1932.

The Judge and I exchanged several telegrams during the month of February. I sent my final one on February 24:

YOUR WIRE DOES NOT EXPLAIN ANYTHING DEFINITELY ABOUT CONTRACT MY ATTITUDE TOWARD THE MATTER IS UNCHANGED

At this point, the genial Judge referred the problem to Braves Vice President Charles F. Adams, to do the tough talking. Adams sent this ultimatum via telegraph on February 25:

COMMUNICATIONS PASSING BETWEEN YOU AND JUDGE FUCHS HAVE BEEN REFERRED TO ME ATTITUDE OF CLUB HAS BEEN MOST CONSIDERATE AND HAS GUARANTEED FAIR TREAT-MENT I HAVE DECIDED THAT A BALL PLAYER IRRESPECTIVE OF HIS ABILITY WHO DOES NOT RESPOND TO SUCH COMPLETE ASSURANCES BY HIS EMPLOYER IS BADLY ADVISED OR BE-LONGS IN SOME OTHER WALK OF LIFE IF YOU DO NOT REPORT ON TIME UNDER CONDITIONS OFFERED YOU WILL BE PLACED ON INELIGIBLE LIST FOR VIOLATION OF CONTRACT NEITHER TRADED NOR SOLD AT ANY PRICE AND ANY DELAY IN REPORT-ING WILL BE DEDUCTED FROM CONTRACT OFFERED YOU AND YOU WILL BEAR EXPENSE OF NECESSARY TRAINING TO GET INTO CONDITION

CHARLES F ADAMS
TRUSTEE AND VICE PRESIDENT BOSTON BRAVES

They had the power to do exactly what Adams threatened. In addition, they could fine me $200 per day for missing spring training. I finally surrendered and signed for $9,000, with the promise, of course, of having the cut restored if the Braves' attendance reached 650,000 in 1933.

It was true that my statistics were not as good in 1932 as they had been during the previous season. However, no player who is hitting over .300 expects to take a cut in salary. It's damn hard to hit .300 consistently in organized baseball on any level, and it's particu-

WALLY, FLU-RIDDEN, IS SENT IN TO PINCH-HIT
WITH BASES LOADED. HE BELTS A HOME RUN,
EARNING WORLD SERIES MONEY FOR HIS TEAM.

larly tough in the majors.

I wasn't thinking about a big raise, but I thought I would get some increase. I remember reading in *Baseball Magazine* in 1940 that I was one of only ten players then in the league with a lifetime average of .300 or better.

The Judge may have been telling the truth when he said that the stockholders had not received any dividends or interest on their investment. However, I read in *Baseball Magazine* for January, 1933 (page 358) that "the Boston Braves was one of the few clubs this past year that made money."

I also read in the Boston papers that Judge Fuchs was paid $5,000 per month as President of the Braves. Judge Landis made a reduction of his pay from $60,000 per year to $40,000. They could afford a cut.

(Footnote to the 1933 Season:)

On August 25, Judge Fuchs sent another "My dear Walter" letter, restoring the cut made in February. The fact that Wally was selected as center fielder on the first National League All-Star Team, and also on the "All-America Team" as the outstanding center fielder in baseball, may have had something to do with it.

Moreover, *Baseball Magazine* reported in September that the Braves had had a good season financially. The same issue contained a quote from Manager McKechnie: "Berger is my only real slugger." He went on to attribute the prosperity of the Braves to Wally's long-distance hitting.

D. Ultimatum from Judge Fuchs, 1934

Without question, Wally was the outstanding center fielder in baseball in 1933. He was the overwhelming choice of the fans in the National League for the first All-Star Game in Chicago. He was the selection of the committee which picked Babe Ruth's All-America Team. *Baseball Magazine* placed him in center field on both their All-Star National League Baseball Club and their All-America Baseball Club.

He was number two in home runs with 27, just one behind Chuck Klein, although he had played in sixteen fewer games because of injuries and illnesses. However, he was first in home run percentage (the number of home runs per 100 times at bat) with 5.1, compared to 4.6 for Klein.

In slugging percentage, Wally was number two, with .566. He was number two in total bases with 299, number two in RBI's with 106, number five in doubles with 37, number six in runs scored with 84 and number nine in batting average with .313.

Two home runs in one game by one batter were registered twenty times in the National League during the 1933 season. Both Berger and Klein performed this feat three times.

The grand climax of his brilliant season came in the final game of the season while he was recuperating from the flu. He changed from his street clothes into a uniform to pinch-hit with the bases loaded. He hit a home run, making the score Boston 4, Philadelphia 1, putting Boston in fourth place and earning $7,000 in World Series money for the team (the share that year for the fourth-place team).

Economic note: Harold Kaese, in his book, *The Boston Braves* (G. P. Putnam's Sons, 1948), reported: "The flame of baseball interest in Boston burned brightly in 1933. Not only did the Braves finish in the first division for the first time in twelve years, but they were in strong contention for the pennant until the last month, when they lost a crucial series to the Giants in Boston...the Braves set an attendance record for themselves by playing to 517,803 fans at home, even though the depression was still on. The big series with the Giants alone drew 150,000 fans to Braves Field."

A health note: Wally played out the season despite having occasional attacks of appendicitis. When the season was over, he had his appendix removed.

In appreciation of the aforementioned efforts and achievements, the President of the Braves offered him a raise of $1,500 for the 1934 season.

After the 1933 season, I decided not to drive West. We planned to stay in Boston for the fall and then drive to Miami and spend the winter there until it was time for spring training. However, I had another mild attack of appendicitis, so I decided not to delay surgery any longer. I went into St. Elizabeth's Hospital for the operation, which was performed by Dr. M. E. McGarty, our team doctor.

Among the visitors at the hospital during my stay there (they kept you in the hospital ten days back then) was Judge Fuchs.

With him was the Mayor of Boston, James Michael Curley.

(His honor, Mayor Curley, was a popular politician in Massachusetts for forty years. At different times, he had been in the state legislature and Congress. Later, he was Governor of Massachusetts, then a Congressman and finally Mayor again.

I read in the paper that Curley was sent to Federal Prison in 1947, but that President Truman let him out. He returned to his job as Mayor until 1950. In that year Truman gave him a full pardon. He ran for Mayor again and lost – of course, by this time, he was getting up there. At the age of seventy-six, he retired from politics.)

The Mayor and the Judge made friendly conversation. The Judge asked me how I was feeling, and so on – and then, finally, he said in a concerned way, "Wally, are we taking care of it?" Meaning, of course, was the club paying the cost of the operation? In those days, there was no Blue Cross or anything like that.

I answered quickly, "Not yet, you haven't, but you'll hear from me whatever the bill is!" When I got out of the hospital, they presented me with a bill for $475. I protested to Dr. McGarty, "Everyone gets their appendix taken out at Massachusetts General for $75--how come it's costing me so much?"

The doctor replied, "Wally, I get as much as $2,500 for that kind of operation."

"Yeah, but you're getting it from some millionaire."

"Come on, Wally, you're making pretty good money."

"Well," I said, "maybe you know what I'm making, but I have only a short time to make it – and I'm trying to put away some money. This is kind of high." Anyway, the club finally refunded the money to me.

It was unusually cold that fall in Boston. Even the Cape Cod Canal froze over. I suggested to my wife that we head for Florida. Duffy Lewis, the team coach, was staying in Miami and he told us there were vacant apartments down there.

I was still on the mend, so my wife drove us in our new Model A, for which I had paid less than a thousand dollars. In Miami, I immediately got in with a bunch of ballplayers down on 16th Street. That's why I negotiated with Judge Fuchs from Miami that year.

On January 17, he sent me a letter which contained a contract offering me $11,500; I refused this offer and asked for $15,000.

January 17, 1934

Dear Walter:

I enclose contract for $11,500.

I am endeavoring to be fair with each individual player and recognize your improvement last year. As soon as business conditions change, I hope to continue to improve the status of the men who are giving us the benefit of their ability, loyalty, skill and hustle.

Please sign and return the contract, for I hope you feel that my action entitles me to no further controversy, and if anything, your approval.

After waiting a week, I sent the unsigned contract back to Judge Fuchs with this letter:

January 25, 1934

Dear Judge:

Am returning contract unsigned. I can not see my way clear to accept the terms therein.

Have been with the Braves for four years, played regular, hustled at all times and was leaned on to furnish the punch for the club. I believe I've lived up to everything a ball club would want of me.

Not being egotistical, I ranked next to Klein in several departments and cannot see where he is worth twice as much in salary than myself. I am as good a hitter as he (Klein) if not a better one. I know that I have outhit him in practically all the parks away from the bandbox at Philly. Do not forget that I have to do most of my hitting in the toughest ball park in the National League.

Judge, I do not feel like I am asking too much when I ask for a contract calling for $15,000 for the coming season.

Hoping to hear favorably from you, I am,

Sincerely yours,
Walter Berger.

In his reply on January 30, it was clear that the Judge took personally my refusal of his contract offer. He got quite emotional, insisting that his proposal represented an increase of $2,500. Actually, my salary was cut from $10,000 to $9,000, then the cut of $1,000 was restored in August. In fact, he was offering me only $1,500 more.

January 30, 1934

Dear Walter:

I am not going into extensive communication. Last year, under conditions which, owing to a change of authority, were dealt with by Mr. Adams, he, knowing the financial situation throughout the country, and also our own condition, saw fit to deduct $1,000 from your previous contract, and you signed it.

When I was returned to authority, I gave you back that cut. Under the agreement made by Mr. Adams, there was no obligation to return it.

Up until 1934, the Judge and I had never discussed contracts and negotiations with the press until we reached a settlement. This year he took his case to the newspapers. I didn't think it was good policy to tell anything to sportswriters. That's not the way I thought we should fight it.

I thought the business was between me and the owners of the ball club. If a reporter asked me if I had signed, I'd just say, "No, we're still arguing." I learned my lesson not to tell them too much. You give a sportswriter a couple of words and he makes a big story out of it.

That accounts for the Associated Press story. The Judge released his statement attacking me, and used that favorite word of owners to describe a player who disagrees with them: "I believe that Berger has been *ill-advised.*"

"I believe that we can come to a fair understanding, but I will not countenance such a stupid, obstinate, unreasonable attitude, and if Berger chooses to maintain that attitude, the Boston club will have to do without his services.

"I have never before discussed the business relationship between the players and the club, but I feel I owe it to the Boston fans to acquaint them with this situation, which has been properly reported by memebers of the press.

"I believe that Berger has been ill-advised. I have endeavored to be fair and friendly with every player I ever had. My policy and attitude toward the players has always been to increase their salaries in accordance with length of service, and also with regard to ability, even if they did not have a good year. I believe I have done my duty in that direction."

The whole statement is not included here. He repeated

what he had said in his letters and telegrams to me, and he referred to my 1933 performance as a "fairly good year." And again he took personally what to me was just the way things had to be done if a ball player was going to get a salary anywhere near what he should. He said "...if he [Berger] were ten times as great as he is, neither he nor any other ball player will dictate to me."

Ed Cunningham, the Club Secretary, sent me a notice on February 21 to report to St. Petersburg on March 10. I sent my reply to the Judge on February 27 by telegram.

February 25, 1934

Dear Judge:

Received a letter from Ed Cunningham asking me to report for spring practice at St. Petersburg on Mar. the 10th.

I am sorry Judge, but I do not intend to come to St. Pete until I have signed a contract.

Very truly yours,
Walter Berger.

JUST RETURNED TO BOSTON AND FOUND YOUR ULTIMATUM I REGRET YOU ARE NOT GOING TO SIGN A CONTRACT I WOULD RATHER STRUGGLE ALONG WITH PLAYERS OF LESS ABILITY THAN BE DICTATED TO IN FACT I WOULD RATHER QUIT BASEBALL THAN BE PUT IN THE POSITION YOU PUT ME THEREFORE I AM NOT COUNTING ON YOUR SERVICES

EMIL E FUCHS.

On March 14, the Associated Press reported that "Emil Fuchs, Boston Braves President, today notified the slugging Wally Berger, now sulking over his 1934 salary terms in Miami, that he would be fined $250 for every day's training he misses after Friday."

Actually I wasn't sulking; I was playing golf, going to the dog races and lounging at the beach. They asked me to come to spring training and talk. I drove to St.Petersburg from Miami and we started negotiating. In the meantime I was getting in shape and they were paying my room and board.

There were three or four other holdouts that year, but they had reported on time to spring training. The Judge met us all in the manager's room, one at a time. I was the last to go in. The guy before me came out muttering, so I said to myself, "I guess he didn't do so good."

So I had to steel myself. The manager, Bill McKechnie, was with the Judge to exert a little pressure, I suppose. I felt he should have given me a little boost, but he probably couldn't.

Anyway, the Judge started talking about how money could buy more – the cost of living, the price of steak, rents, and so forth. That's when I told him that I didn't give a damn about that. I said, "I only got a short life in baseball, and if you can't pay me what I'm worth now, why don't you trade me to a club that can? I read in the paper that the New York Giants are interested in me. Why don't you send me over there? I should get paid for what I do. If I have a bad year, I expect to get cut. If I have a good year, I expect a raise."

The Judge told me he didn't want to get rid of me. "We can't give you a raise – this is a bad time – we're losing money." And I suppose they were – at least, they weren't making much. You could tell that by the gate. There were a lot of people out of work and crowds were small except on the weekend. I finally signed for $12,000; I don't think I could have really gotten any more, but the press assumed that I got a lot more.

On March 24, LeRoy Atkinson wrote in his column, The Southern Exposure, about his talk with me after I had signed. "Berger signed for an increase in salary – an increase of considerable voltage." It wasn't so considerable. I must have had some second thoughts about signing, because he also reported this remark – which I can't remember making: "What a chump I was to sign," remarked Wally Berger.

E. The Braves on the Brink (1935)

Wally maintained his status as the best center fielder in the National League in 1934, particularly in the eyes of his peers. In a poll of 154 players, coaches and managers, Berger was first with 59 votes, Kiki Cuyler was second with 34 and Chick Hafey was third with fifteen.

Boston sportswriter Joe Cashman contrasted this voting by the professionals with the popular votes of the fans. As their selection for outfielders, they chose Klein, now in Chicago, as number one. Medwick was second, Berger was third and Ott was fourth. Joe Moore, the overwhelming choice of his fellows for the left field position, was not included in the top six by the fans.

Berger finished second in home runs with thirty-four, while

Rip Collins and Mel Ott were tied for first with thirty-five each. It would have been a three-way tie for first if Wally had received credit for a disputed home run which spectators and sportswriters described as a homer – only the umpire saw the ball bounce from the field of play into the stands. By his ruling it was just a double.

Wally was second in extra-base hits (77), third in slugging percentage (.546), third in total bases (336), third in RBIs (121), third in home run percentage (5.5), eighth in doubles (35), eleventh in runs scored (92) and eleventh in hits (183).

His batting average dropped two points below the "magic number" (to .298). Nowhere can it be more clearly demonstrated that batting average alone is only one of the many criteria that should be used to evaluate the effectiveness of a hitter.

Berger was more effective, for example, in four important categories than Paul Waner, who led the National League with .362, and Bill Terry, who was second with .354. Wally – with his .298 average – was only number twenty-nine among players in one hundred games or more, but his effectiveness was very great, as can be readily observed in this comparison:

Extra Base Hits:	Berger, 77; Waner, 62; Terry, 23.
Total Bases:	Berger, 336; Waner, 323; Terry, 279.
Home Runs:	Berger, 34; Waner, 14; Terry, 8.
Runs Batted In:	Berger, 121; Waner, 90; Terry, 83.
Slugging Percentage:	Berger, .546; Waner, .539; Terry, .463.

Wally was busy out in center field, as well. He was second to Lloyd ("Little Poison") Waner of Pittsburgh in total chances. Waner had 422 to Wally's 403. Chick Hafey was third with 400.

Within a week after I received my contract in 1935, I mailed it back to Judge Fuchs. I agreed to the amount he offered – $12,000. It was the first time since I had been sold to Boston that I signed immediately. All of us on the Braves knew that the club was in trouble when they cut an order for twelve bats down to six!

The Judge mentioned in his letter of January 28 that they were refinancing the club and that "there would be no future danger of holding up even small bills." He was referring to a bill which I had submitted to him earlier.

In an article I clipped from a Boston newspaper titled "Tribal Losses in 1934," the correspondent reported, "According to the annual statement of condition filed with the Secretary of the Commonwealth, the 1934 Braves went into red ink to the extent of $44,308." The article also said that the Braves had re-negotiated their annual stadium lease, down from $40,000 to $36,667. Player contracts for the season amounted to $98,534. (All major league teams carried twenty-five players, giving some idea of what they were paying the average ball player during the depression years.)

It was the last year that I argued with the Judge. I didn't know it at the time, but in August, according to the *Reach Official Baseball Guide* for 1936, "Judge Fuchs severed his connection with the Club and the franchise was virtually operated by the National League until mid-winter, when it was sold to Robert Quinn, former Red Sox President and later business manager at Brooklyn."

F. Exit Judge Fuchs – Enter Bob Quinn

"No major team started the season with more hurrah than the Braves. Just when the teams were ready to go to training camp, Boston announced its coup of having signed Babe Ruth.

"When the season opened, Ruth began his National League career by hitting his 709th home run at the expense of Carl Hubbell of the Giants. It the looked as if the Braves were set.

"Compared with the gala opening, the close of the season was a tragedy. Ruth was gone and the Braves were in last place, 26 behind the seventh-place Phillies. Moreover, the Braves lost 115 games during the year, the worst showing by a tailender since 1899, when Cleveland lost 134 games for a record." *(Reach Official Baseball Guide for 1936.)*

After this disaster, Wally had to deal with a new personality in his annual bargaining. The Judge was gone, and in his place was Bob Quinn, business manager of the Brooklyn Dodgers the previous two years. Quinn was an old-timer who had been an executive in the majors since 1917 with the St. Louis Browns, the Boston Red Sox (which under his leadership finished in last place eight times in ten years) and the Dodgers.

Wally had some good arguments for the new president in his attempt to squeeze out a raise for 1936. For the third year in a row, he had been selected for the National League All-Star Team. He was also the new home run king of the League, with 34 homers. (Ott was second with 31 and Camilli was third with twenty-five.) In addition, he played the role of the fictional "Frank Merriwell" a number of times – three of which are summarized below:

"The mightiest stroke any batsman can perform is to blast a home run with the bases loaded. This was done to the number of forty-three times in the majors in 1935; on twenty-five occasions in the American League and eighteen in the National.

Home run bomber number one with the bases full was Wally Berger of the Boston Braves, who performed the feat three times." *(Reach, 1936)*

Wally was number one in home run percentage (5.8), number one in RBI's (130), number three in total bases (323), number four in slugging percentage (.548), and number six in two-baggers.

Moreover, he was the busiest outfielder in baseball, with 458 putouts and 483 total chances. In the National League, Ethan Allan was second with 412 and 447, respectively. Over in the American League, Sammy West was the leader with 449 and 461.

For his unstinting and unflagging effort the whole year long with a last-place team, President Bob Quinn offered Wally a $500 raise, from $12,000 to $12,500. Wally refused the offer and reminded Quinn of his accomplishments of the preceding season. Quinn replied with the most egregious (no other adjective will do to describe the statement) nonsense ever uttered by a club president in the history of baseball bargaining:

"I know you hit in 130 runs, and if you go through the files of *The Sporting News* (if you keep a file), you will find that a lot of the runs that you hit in did not mean a thing. I do not say this now to hurt your feelings. I am only telling you the gospel truth. You know the club won only 38 ball games, and any man hitting in 130 runs should win more games than that himself."

Wally's response to Quinn's insulting letter was a masterpiece of restraint:

Quinn sent me a contract on January 31, 1936. Naturally, I was expecting a good raise since I had led the league in home runs and runs batted in. His offer of only a $500 increase really shocked me. I immediately made a counter-offer, asking for a $5,000 raise.

Quinn, who had been around baseball for over forty years, was "surprised" that I didn't jump at his generous offer. The appendix includes the complete exchange of letters because they show how management tried to "con" the players. They must have thought that we were really simple-minded.

Often while I was playing for Boston, the sports writers would say that my long-distance hitting helped to draw the crowds to the Boston park. I don't know whether Bob Quinn read it or not, but in late June of 1936, writer John Brooks wrote an article about me in which I was described as "the box-office home run hitter." It covered a half-page, including a record of my at-bats and home runs from April 25 until June 20. Here are some quotations taken from that article:

"Four home runs in the past week, five circuit clouts in the last five playing days, have made Berger the gauge by which other money hitters are measured.

"Playing in exhausting double headers day after day, double headers which have stopped the league leaders in their tracks, Berger has staged the most vicious batting splurge of his big league career.

"...for Wally is the answer to the magnate's box office prayer. It's his thundering bat, which booming at such dramatically chosen moments, is helping to lift the Tribe out of the cellar. It's the report of Wally's terrific battering which has started the Wigwam turnstiles clicking after long weeks of disuse. It is *Wally* (italics added) who is the big selling point for prospective buyers as the Tribal ownership is offered about the league – so far with no buyers in sight."

Brooks was an impartial judge who wrote what he observed and believed. I didn't know him, and can't remember ever being interviewed by him. Maybe I should have saved this clipping for Bob Quinn (not really). At a meeting on March 6, he convinced me that they couldn't pay more, wouldn't pay more and wouldn't trade me to a club which might pay more.

Hal Lee, who had a good year in 1935, batting .303, was also holding out for a raise. We both surrendered on March 6 at St. Petersburg. After we signed, Quinn told the press that I was "a very likeable young man and one who is possessed of considerable common sense." He must have still been sore at Lee because Hal's name wasn't included in that compliment. My salary for 1936 was $12,500, the highest I ever made in the major leagues.

"I signed the contract for $10,000. This was still the Depression and it was still pretty good money."

SEVEN

FROM BOSTON TO
NEW YORK
TO CINCINNATI

A. Good-Bye, Boston – Hello, New York (1937)

Recovered completely from his broken hand, Wally hit the ball hard in spring training in 1937, including "One of the hardest hits in the history of Waterfront Park," according to "Sunshine Al" Lang, the former mayor, who had been watching big league exhibition games there for twenty-five years.

Burt Whitman wrote that "Berger gave the ball a ride that would have made it clear the left center wall at Alston (Braves' Field) in Boston."

Berger played in the city series against the Red Sox and his old high school teammate, Joe Cronin. He hit a home run in the second game, which writer Joe Cashman described with his usual colorful adjectives: "Only an inning later, Moore hit safely with two down and then Berger's fearful home run smash added two to the Bees' count." (Note that the Braves have become the Bees.)

However, on the opening day against Philadelphia, he had another bit of bad luck, breaking a finger trying to handle a line drive and missing the first month of play as a result. Right fielder Gene Moore was hit by a pitched ball in the Red Sox series and was also out of action, resulting in two-thirds of the regular outfield being on the injured list.

In mid-May both Moore and Berger were back, and on May 21, at Pittsburgh, they each had two doubles and a triple to outhit and outscore the Pirates. At that time, in discussing a possible trade for Berger, John Brooks wrote: "As Berger went, so went the Bees. The Bees won four straight – and Berger, in five games, hit .388. At bat eighteen times, he made seven hits, four for extra bases."

There had been rumors of a Berger trade all season. McKechnie admitted that he would trade Berger if he thought it would help the club. It was widely reported that Berger was going to Pittsburgh, but on June 15 he was traded to New York. The Giants, of course, paid him the salary imposed upon him in Boston the previous winter.

Wally alternated in the outfield for the Giants for the first time in his major league career since he had established himself with the Braves in 1930. Although he got into 89 games, he played in the field in only eighty. Times at bat tell the story. In 1935, he was at bat 589 times; in 1936, 534 times; however, in 1937, only 312 times. Manager Terry used him mainly against left-handed pitchers, but he might have acted differently if computers had been around to provide him with instant data. Wally had always been quite effective against right-handers.

Despite irregular play, Wally was again much more effective than his .285 average indicated to the average fan. Moreover, he came through for the Giants, often in true "Merriwell" fashion, in the most critical period of the season, and was a vital force in their winning the championship of the National League.

He got 89 hits in 312 times at bat, but of those 89 hits, forty were for extra bases. His total bases numbered 166. He batted in 65 runs and scored 54, a total of 102 runs accounted for. Only five other hitters got more than the 17 home runs that Wally hit. Medwick, the home run leader with 31, was at bat 633 times, for example. (This is not to disparage in any way Medwick's tremendous achievement; he had an incredible season and was in first place in seven of the nine statistical categories that relate to hits and runs scored.)

Wally was number two in home run percentage with 5.5, but it is not so indicated in the *Baseball Encyclopedia*, because he did not play in one hundred games; nor is he listed number five in slugging percentage (with .532) for the same reason.

He was voted a full share of the World Series money, of course, in addition to his salary, which amounted to $4489.95, and which in 1937 supplied considerable purchasing power.

When negotiating time came in January of 1938, Bill Terry, the old holdout himself, was now on the other side of the fence. As the leader of the management team, Manager Terry cut Wally's pay by $2,500, back to $10,000. Terry was in the "$20,000 bracket" himself, according to *Baseball Magazine*. He also played his role well with the invidious comment in his letter of February 1, that "I am sure you agree with me that the amount both the Boston and New York Clubs paid you for services rendered was very much out of line..." And he did not mean that Wally was underpaid!

Terry may have still remembered and may have still been smarting over an article in *Baseball Magazine* which made an unflattering comparison of his batting record to Wally's ("The Run-Makers," by Hal Rosey, February, 1936).

Wally did not take offense. He merely assumed that Terry was doing his job for the owners. Wally liked and respected Terry, and, in his own words, knew he was "getting up there." After all, he was 33 years old and in the ninth year of his major league career!

After I was with the Giants for a while, I finally adjusted myself to New York and the way Terry handled things. For instance, he figured that I wouldn't hit right-handed pitchers as well as his left-handed batters, but sometimes he was wrong. One day a guy named Frey was pitching against us and when Gus Mancuso, the captain, read the lineup, I wasn't in it. I said to Mancuso, "How come?"

He said, "Frey's pitching and Terry thinks because of his side-arm curve ball, you won't hit him.

"Frey," I said, "I can hit him like I own him. That's my cousin! For Christ's sake, why doesn't he ask me?"

Actually, I didn't care to hit left-handers so much. The only left-handers I saw were the best in baseball. Opposing teams didn't pitch their mediocre left-handers against us because we were a right-handed hitting club – and I had always hit well against right-handed pitchers.

Anyway, I played in and out according to the manager's pleasure, and when it came down to the end, we were in first place, I had helped win it. I won some key games for them, and in a race like that, each game is big. When I hit a pinch homer to win a game, it meant something. I helped and the players appreciated me.

Since I had joined the Giants after the season began, the players had to vote on me for the World Series cut. If you're there all year, you automatically get a full share. I remember before they had their meeting to decide, Jimmy Ripple, a good hustling ball player, one of the other outfielders, came up to me and said, "Wally, they'd better give you a full share because when I'm in that meeting,

I'm going to raise hell if they don't. I'm going to make myself heard!"

When the meeting was over, Jimmy reported to me that I got a full share by a unanimous vote. There wasn't any one guy in there saying, "Nah, he ain't worth that," or "He shouldn't get that." In my heart I thought I was entitled to it because I had hit good enough and had played all the outfield positions.

B. Bargaining With the Old Holdout Himself, Bill Terry (1938)

On December 29, 1937, Terry sent me a contract for 1938 with a cut from $12,500 to $10,000. His stationery indicated that he was both General Manager and Field Manager of the Giants. In my response of January 6, 1938, I returned my contract unsigned and told him that I didn't expect a cut of that size.

In my postscript to that letter I assured him that my injured finger had healed, but President Horace Stoneham sent me a letter dated January 24, asking me to make an appointment for a physical examination by Doctor Fish on West Sixth Street in Los Angeles.

On February 1, 1938, Terry enclosed the same contract and made the statement that my pay had been out of line in Boston; he was suggesting that I had been overpaid. That didn't bother me, because he had tried on several occasions to convince Judge Fuchs to sell me to New York, and I had always given the Giants trouble when I was playing with Boston – that is, unless Hubbell was pitching. Terry also hinted that my arm might be bad and that I would have to prove to him in spring training that it was o.k.

I signed the contract for $10,000. This was still the depression and it was still pretty good money. There were a few players who made more, but there weren't many above me. I wanted to go back with a good frame of mind, to report to spring training and bear down and beat Hank Leiber for center field.

That was my idea. I'd had my bum arm worked on the year before and it was all right. I bore down in spring training. I got into good shape and played in a lot of games in which I hit well. In fact, I led the Giants in hitting in spring training with an average around .400.

However, when the regular season started, I rode the bench most of the time. On June 6, I was traded to Cincinnati, putting me back with my old manager from Boston, Bill McKechnie, who had moved to the Reds the year after I left Boston.

102

> **BERGER TRADED FOR KAMPOURIS**
>
> Cincinnati, June 7 (AP) Wally Berger, the hard hitting out-fielder, who formerly established records in a Boston Bees uniform, was back with the skipper today as a Redleg.
>
> In a trade with the New York Giants, Berger was exchanged yesterday for second sacker Alex Kampouris. Everybody appeared satisfied, for Manager Bill Terry had sought frantically for a second baseman at every stop on his western tour...

C. Exchanges With The Wily Warren Giles (1939)

Warren C. Giles, Vice President and General Manager of the Cincinnati team, showed a fine knack for mixing disparagement with praise in his contract letter of November 22, 1938, in which he offered Wally a salary of $10,000 for the 1939 season. This was the same amount he had received in his settlement with the Giants the previous year.

Three times in three short paragraphs, Giles inserted disparaging digs. In paragraph two, he put in this one: "While you are probably not the great ball player you were when this high salary was established..." It was a calculated device to make a player in his tenth year feel insecure. After all, the average career life of a major league ball player was four-and-one-half years, and every veteran knew it.

In paragraph three, he speaks for both himself and Manager McKechnie when we writes, "...while Bill and I were both disappointed that you did not hold up..." But on the other hand, Giles continues, "...we were well-satisfied."

In the fourth paragraph, Giles pays deference to the fetish of the .300 batting average, which incidentally, even the players tend to believe in. Giles intones, "You will agree (Management was always saying, "You will agree...) that it is a little unusual for a club like Cincinnati to pay a salary of $10,000 a year to an outfielder whose hitting record is not considerably in excess of .300."

Wally's average for that year is listed in the *Baseball Encyclopedia* at .307, his record for games he played with Cincinnati. In the *Spalding Guide,* he is recorded at .2984, his combined average with New York and Cincinnati.

Of course, Giles sent "kind personal regards" and "wishes for a pleasant winter."

Actually, Giles averred that they were really offering that exorbitant sum because of Wally's disposition, conduct and hustle. What General Manager Giles didn't mention was that Wally and company had drawn 750,000 paying customers into the park that year to set a new attendance record at Crosley Field, and that the fans came to the park to see feats like these:

July 9: "Blonde Wally's four-master in the opening round carried into the left field bleachers above the 375-foot mark, while his fourth round homer carried completely over the bleachers." (Homers #5 and #6.)

July 10: "Berger's third homer in two days was a mighty wallop. It carried in a line over the left field bleacher wall and bounded through an open window on the far side of the street." (Homer #7)

July 16: "It has been a long time since the fans saw such a tremendous home run as that made by Wally Berger in the fourth inning. The ball sailed far over the high sign on the roof of the laundry across York Street and cleared the entire building. An employee of the laundry climbed to the roof of the structure, but he could not find the sphere." (Homer #8)

October 2: "Wally Berger's 15th homer of the year over the left field wall in the eighth round, proved to be the game winning marker." Last game of the season: Cincinnati 5, Pittsburgh 4. Winning pitcher: Vander Meer.

A realistic evaluation of a major league player must always be related to the situation in the league in that season and to the conditions of work which the player encountered. Obviously, management focuses on those aspects which are unfavorable to the player in the bargaining situation and ignores those which are favorable.

In 1938, Wally did not really begin the season until he arrived in Cincinnati on June 7, so that he played in only 115 games. For the season in Cincinnati he batted .307, but counting his very infrequent play in New York, his batting average was .2984 for the season.

Wally was then number eighteen in batting average, but he was number eight in slugging percentage with .478. Out of a total of thirty-two regular outfielders in the National League, he was number six in batting average and number four in slugging percentage. Only seven hitters hit more home runs – and every one of them played in at least thirty more games. Wally batted in sixty runs while hitting in the number-two spot in the batting order, and he scored 79 runs.

Batting order is very important, and so is speed. Lombardi, who led the league in batting average, for instance, hit into thirty double plays. He was very slow getting down to first base, or getting that extra base on a long hit.

Wally signed quickly for $10,000, ignoring the infelicitous comments from Giles and retorting amiably that "The terms were very satisfactory and I appreciate the fact that you and Bill were satisfied with my work of last season."

On opening day he put Leiber out there. I was mad as hell. I knew I had won that damn job, but there was a feud going on between Leiber and Terry. Leiber didn't like Terry. He had held out for $12,000 – he had played well the previous season, hitting 27 home runs. Terry wasn't going to give him twelve thousand bucks and he finally had to sign for ten. So he didn't want to play for Terry and he used to fake it, but Terry made him play.

From the very beginning of the season there were rumors that Terry was going to trade me. Terry needed a second baseman. Kampouris was playing second for Cincinnati, but they wanted a left fielder. I don't think McKechnie cared much for Kampouris, although he was a good ball player. It may have been his attitude.

When we were playing the Reds in Cincinnati, I knew McKechnie was watching. I knew he was wondering about my throwing arm, so I showed off when I was out on the field shagging flies. When I threw the ball back to the guy receiving it for the fungo batter, I'd cut it loose and throw it pretty good. I think that made up McKechnie's mind that my arm was all right, so they made the trade.

By the first of June in 1938, I had played in only nine regular games, despite the fact that I'd had a great spring training. I had played in every game. Just before the opening of the season, we played at West Point. I hit one clear out of sight over a building in left field. All the cadets sitting around were excited, but it didn't impress Terry at all.

They traded us even up, player for player, with no money involved. Of course, when you make a deal like that in the middle of the year, it's the same contract.

I went to Cincinnati and started over again looking for a place to live: first a hotel and then you ask the other ball players where there's a good place to live. I was back with Bill McKechnie.

I did all right the rest of the season with the Reds, finishing the season with a pretty good record. Then I had to deal with the next contract. Giles sent me a contract for the same amount. I was probably betting that I would get the same money as the Giants had given me. I played the next year for $10,000, which was still pretty good pay.

1930 - 1940

THE END OF THE LINE

EIGHT

FROM CINCINNATI TO PHILADELPHIA TO INDIANAPOLIS TO LOS ANGELES

A. Going Down (1939-40)

On October 10, 1939, Wally Berger was thirty-four years old. He had just completed his tenth year of work in the National League. A quick leafing through the pages of *The Baseball Encyclopedia* reveals that the careers of most players end when they reach their mid-thirties, regardless of the period in which they played. A Rabbit Maranville, Ty Cobb or a Willie McCovey is a rare bird, indeed; and a Satchel Paige or a Babe Ruth is regarded as a genetic miracle.

Yet there is great variation in the rate at which people age. It may be that management and player sometimes become part of a self-fulfilling prophecy. This means that by believing and predicting that a player is over the hill at thirty-five, they help to make the prediction come true.

Management may detect decline in every miscue, every slump of a veteran player. And the player himself may accept such definitions and act as if they were true, also. This may have been the case with Wally.

Of course, there are other obvious factors. Promising young replacements are waiting in the wings; they will be more enthusiastic and much cheaper – at least that's the way it was in 1939.

General Manager Giles made a passing reference to young Mike McCormick of Indianapolis, "On whom we get very promising reports, and in whom we have quite an investment." He also mentioned that in his correspondence with other clubs, they said

107

that "They were directing their efforts toward securing younger players."

Giles made no bones about economic concerns. In his first letter he stated bluntly, "Your performance on the field is getting to a point where you cannot expect more than the salary I am offering." In his letter of January 10, 1940, he discussed the average pay of the Cincinnati outfielders and concluded: "In other words, we would not want to pay $6,500 to a player when we felt we could get the same performance from someone at $4,500 or $5,000."

Two significant differences in the bargaining of that era from that of the present can be detected in the Berger/Giles exchange of 1939-40. First, there was the personal nature of that kind of individual bargaining. Giles wrote at length discussing and justifying his stand. Wally countered with his explanations and arguments from his point of view.

Second, as they dickered over the salary, both parties knew that the salary agreed upon might be very temporary. Management could offer a salary that it did not have to pay unless it chose to do so. The player could be released at any time unconditionally and receive pay for only ten days of the contract. The contrast today is very marked. An ordinary player, a designated hitter, received his release last year, and management was obliged to pay off his $200,000 contract.

Wally was now fighting for survival. Knowing that he might be cut loose after the season was under way, he asked Giles to give him his release that winter so that he could deal with other clubs that might need an experienced outfielder; thus he would have been able to start the season afresh. Giles wouldn't do it. For his own reasons he left Wally hanging.

In his own words, Wally had a "rotten season." These words were spoken in a moment of disappointment and they were only partly true. If he had been trained in collective bargaining at the Harvard Business School, he would not have admitted to any such thing. Instead, he would have conceded that he got off to a very slow start, and would have emphasized that from mid-July to early October, when the St. Louis Cardinals were chasing them, he came on strong and helped Cincinnati win the pennant.

He might also have sent Giles some clippings. On August 4, a reporter wrote, "Wally is currently hitting the ball harder than anyone in the league." A picture on the sports page on September

29 showed Wally sliding home with the "pennant-clinching run." "Berger's sixth round double smacked right alongside No. 22, his number on the scoreboard...he scored the winning run after doubling, in the most important game of the season."

Wally was batting only .209 in May. He started to get warm in July, and in August he really got hot. He replaced Craft, who was injured, and was put back in his old familiar spot in center field.

Yet it was his poorest season – statistically – in his professional career. He was way down the list of batting averages with .258, but his slugging percentage was a healthy .4376, making him number twenty-three out of eighty players who had been in 75 or more games. In ninety-seven games he hit fourteen home runs (Mize, the league leader, hit 28 in 153 games). He scored 36 runs, batted in forty-four and accounted for 144 total bases.

Wally went hitless in the World Series. Giles could not resist mentioning it in a highly subjective way: "I do not know exactly how to express this to you, but you are the kind of fellow who seems to go better when the fans are 'in your corner,' and I must say that some plays in the World Series games have had an effect of alienating the fans' affections in the case of two or three ball players on the club, and one of them unfortunately is you." Actually, it seemed that Giles had an excessive talent for expressing insults in a less than subtle fashion.

Again Koppet's reminder that "statistics merely count what has already happened; they say nothing about why." It is when the statistics in baseball become flesh and blood and muscle that the aficionado of the sport gains insight into the play.

Giles didn't bother to mention that Wally was "a great factor down the stretch as he was two years ago when he helped to propel the Giants to a pennant." Nor did he mention that the 1939 Series was not exactly a slug-fest. The entire Cincinnati team hit for 32 total bases in 37 innings of play. In the mighty Yankees' lineup, Crosetti hit .063, Rolfe hit .125, Selkirk hit .167, Gordon hit .143, and Dahlgren hit .214. The batting average for the Yankee squad was .206; for Cincinnati, .203.

For a .258 batter, Wally provided some spectacular feats for the fans in 1939, and perhaps won their temporary affection. Even a foul ball which he hit was worth reporting. It was the longest one recorded in the park's history, as it carried for 550 feet.

Some samples: "Berger then picked out that laundry across

York Street as a target for abuse and his belt caromed off one of the sign's supports on the roof and dropped into the street...

"He smashed two tremendous home runs, each with a man on board, to account for four runs...

"...booming double off the left field wall that drove home the tying run in the ninth...

"Berger's sixth home run of the season was a mighty swat., It carried high over the left field wall onto the roof of the laundry building, a wallop of some 400 feet...

"Berger's fifth homer in his last six games and his eleventh of the season was probably his longest of the year. He got it up into the high wind sweeping into left field and it carried over the bleachers some 400 feet from the plate...

"...a terrific smack that landed on the roof of the laundry across York Street...

"...it collided with the top of the sign on top of the laundry (grand slam)...

Wally's September/October finish in 1939:

September 13: one for one, including a home run.

September 18: two for four.

September 20: three for four.

September 22: two for six, including a home run.

September 23: three for six, including two doubles and
a home run.

September 26: three for six, including a triple.

September 28: one for two, aforementioned double scoring the winning run and winning the championship of the National League.

October 1: in Pittsburgh, the last game that the regulars played before the Series, Wally had two for five, including a double, drove in two runs, had five put-outs on the field, and stole one base...hardly an indication of senility.

All the letters in the negotiations of 1940 are included. The opening offer in Giles' letter of December 29, 1939, was for a salary of $5,500, representing a cut of almost fifty per cent.

Wally pointed out that management always seemed to want to have it both ways: They offer a small increases when a player has a good year, and propose enormous cuts when a player has a poor season.

It was clear that a player bargaining individually was virtually powerless. The cards were all stacked in favor of management, and Giles made it obvious that while baseball may be only a game to the fans, to management it was often a cruel, hard business in which they ask the players: "What have you done for me lately?"

In February, Giles raised his offer to $7,250. He arrived at this figure "by striking an average of the salaries of the outfielders already signed on our club." In fairness he said that he did not include Luce and Galatzer. This was quite a concession, since Luce never played in a major league game, and Galatzer was at bat exactly five times in 1939 and never played another game. On February 19, 1940, Wally signed for $7,250.

When Warren Giles sent me a contract for $5,500 for the 1940 season, I was expecting a cut, but nothing like that. I had hit only .258, but I did win some key games for them and really helped the Reds win the league championship. Therefore, I didn't accept the contract. I told him that they didn't raise anybody four or five thousand dollars – how come you cut me $4,500?

Giles was reared in the Branch Rickey School, the St. Louis Cardinals' organization, and he had some of Rickey's qualities in attempting to get you cheap. He was more like a politician. He would grin all the time, but he was cold. Not like Judge Fuchs. He was easier to talk to. He was a little sentimental, and he wanted to be liked, but he tried sort of business-like to get you cheap, too.

By the middle of February, Giles had raised the ante to $7,250. I figured that I wasn't going to get any more anyway, and I thought that if I got to play and played regularly, I could bounce back. Also, we had a great team, so I was thinking we ought to get into the World Series again.

By the way, what he said in his letter about my doing well, getting the World Series money in addition to my salary, was true. But who did he think was making the money?

In our run for the pennant, we drew big crowds, and it was the fans who paid us the World Series money. The grand total for the four games was $845,329, of which the players (including the share for second, third and fourth place teams) got a little over half to divide up.

Giles didn't need to remind me that I was thirty-five years old – that's old for professional athletes. The reflexes of the average player of 35 do slow down a little bit, even though you don't think so. I admit that I'd be the last one to think that I was through. But I could still move pretty fast. Even at 44 when I was a manager, I ran against some fast kids and they barely beat me.

The writers and the critics are hard on you. They say, "He's slowed down a step." I knew that I hadn't slowed down a step, but when you read that stuff, they leave a little doubt in your mind. It kind of hastens your end. You think, "Maybe I *am* through," and no player wants to be through.

I loved to play the game so much that the one thing that I dreaded was the day I couldn't play anymore. Most all the players were that way. There were probably some who didn't give a damn, but most fellows felt the way I did. They dreaded the day when the guy says you can't play anymore. "Please don't tell me that, coach!"

Giles rubbed it in about my performance in the World Series when I went zero-for-fifteen. You get used to it from the fans because they always expect you to deliver, even though the best hitters in baseball get a hit only once in about every three times at bat. That's on the average.

The '39 Series was a pitcher's series for the most part. Yet Keller, who hit a total of eleven home runs in 111 games, hit three in the last two games of the series. Lonnie Frey, who hit eleven during the regular season (like me), didn't get a hit in the series – and he was a great second baseman and a consistent hitter throughout his career.

Lou Gehrig, one of the greatest hitters who ever played, didn't get a hit in his first three All-Star games. Giles was unfair; as a professional person, he knew better. He was just trying to win points in dickering with me.

Luck is always being discussed in connection with performance in sports. If I had been lucky, I might have had seven hits instead of none. I hit at least seven right on the button. I hit one over the fence and it curved foul. I hit one through the box, and I don't know how Joe Gordon got over there, but he came up with it and threw me out. I hit a line drive toward short. Crosetti leaped up into the air and it hit his glove; instead of bounding away, it went straight up and he caught it coming down. I ducked to get away from an inside pitch and the ball hit my bat and rolled to the pitcher. It just wasn't my series to hit.

The truth is that Giles didn't want to pay me $10,000 when he thought he could get a good young player for $4,500. He liked

Mike McCormick, who was playing that year in the American Association for Indianapolis. He could run fast and was a good outfielder, but he was no power hitter. He hit .318 for Indianapolis, with two home runs for the season.

Galatzer, who was 32 years old, was hitting .325 for Indianapolis and came up for three games with Cincinnati. It was clear to me that I would have to prove to the manager in spring training that I could still play well enough.

B. The End of the Line

Failing to get his release from Giles in the Winter of 1939-40 and receiving the usual notice to report, Wally went to spring training in good faith and in good shape. Because he was a "ten-year man," he could not be sent down to the minors.

Upon arriving at camp, he found himself treated in a manner unworthy of professionals in any vocation. Here, one of the greatest players of the decade, four times selected to the National League All-Star Team, and one who had observed the highest standards of ethical and professional conduct, was now subjected to deliberate humiliation.

In the exhibition games he was never given a chance to play, nor to demonstrate whether his skills were still adequate for major league play. He was not permitted to take batting practice with the regulars. He was sent down to the other end of the field with the "scrubs."

Wally was especially disappointed in his old manager and friend, Bill McKechnie, who collaborated in this treatment. Moreover, Bill never let him know of his impending release, nor discussed it with him when it occurred.

On May 10, 1940, about six weeks into the season, Wally was summoned to the General Manager's office and given his unconditional release. He lost his temper and expressed himself in expletives for the first time in his long dialogue with management in the major leagues, and his behavior was certainly warranted and appropriate.

(Giles didn't even remember to send Wally his ten days' pay upon his release. Wally had to write him to get the $429.76 that he then had coming!)

Wally was able to make a deal with the Phillies for a salary of $7,500. He played infrequently and briefly, although he was hitting .302 after appearing in twenty-two games. Indianapolis of the American Association offered him $2,000 to sign and $500 per month for the remainder of the season.

Montreal of the International League made the same offer. Wally asked Tony Lazzeri, now manager at Montreal, if he could top the bonus offered by Indianapolis. He couldn't, so Wally, who was "going toward the coast," stopped off to play in Indianapolis.

At Indianapolis, Wally's hand was broken by a pickoff throw, and so he went home early to California. He received his release that November, playing briefly for the Angels in 1941 – mainly for sentimental reasons. From there it was World War II with the United States Navy, where his talents were recognized and used in their training program.

During 1940 spring training at Tampa, they didn't play me at all. I never played in the exhibition games. I went down with the "scrubs" at the other end of the field during regular batting practice. I saw the writing on the wall there. I thought, "This is it. He's going to force me right out of baseball." And so it happened.

On May 10, I was at my apartment in Cincinnati with my gear already packed in the trunk. We were going to St. Louis. Giles called me up and said he wanted to see me in his office. I knew right away – they don't usually call your house to tell you to come down to the office.

I went down there and he's sitting in his office smug as a bug and he started talking. He told me what a great asset I'd been to baseball...a credit to the game...that I hustled, that I did this and I did that.

I interrupted and said, "Now, don't hand me that crap, just hand me my goddam release. That's what you called me down for."

He said, "Well, the Yankees need an outfielder..."

I was hot under the collar and said, "Listen, don't bring the Yankees up. If I can't play for you, I sure as hell can't play for the Yankees. Just give me the damn release and let me go on my way." And I left him with that and stormed out of the office.

Of course I didn't like it a bit. The season was well under way. No player likes to be released that way. Everybody's filled up. Unless something happens to an outfielder, he gets hurt or sick, and you're available. But if everybody is in good shape, no one needs you. You're two thousand miles from home, you've rented an apartment, and here's your paycheck, good-bye. Only they forgot to give me the paycheck – I had to write and remind them.

Here I was without a job, but I had money. I wasn't worried about that. The apartment was rented from month to month. We never signed a lease, and we usually left for California at the close of the season. Anyway, I contacted the Phillies (or they contacted me). I got a little better contract from them than I had with the Reds.

When I went to Philadelphia, they had an outfield of Klein, Arnovich, Rizzo, and Joe Marty. None of the outfielders were hitting, but they didn't play me. I wondered why they brought me over there. Finally I got to play, but by this time I'm out of rhythm.

I had been sitting on the bench and I had a different look at baseball then. Doc Prothro was the manager, and I didn't care for his methods. In my mind, I said, "This is for the birds." The Phillies weren't going anywhere, so they gave me my release in July. Now I was three thousand miles from home without a job.

Tony Lazzeri, who was now managing Montreal, sent me a wire offering me a bonus of $2,000 to sign with them. I also got a wire from Jewel Ens at Indianapolis, who made the same offer. I called Tony in Montreal to see if he could up the offer. I knew him well from San Francisco. Tony said he couldn't give me any more, so I told him I'd take Indianapolis. I thought that, since I was heading for the coast, I might as well stop off there, and then I'd be on my way.

As it was, I got to Indianapolis where all the games were played at night except on Sundays. That's why I appreciate and sympathize with the ball player today. You play nights during the week. You play a night game Saturday and jump in a hot country to a double-header during the day on Sunday.

I hadn't played too much night ball. I discovered that your arms feel dead, your legs feel dead. At that pace I didn't have any life, but I did hit good on Sunday. I could see the ball better. Timing was better for me in the daytime. Everything seemed faster at night. I remember batting against Parmalee in the National League. He looked fast, but he seemed extra fast at night. Then when I saw him again in the daytime, he wasn't so fast.

A pickoff play ended my stay in Indianapolis. I was on first base when the catcher threw down there and hit me on the hand. It was broken, and by the time it would have healed, the season would have been nearly over. They let me go home early, and in

November they mailed me my release. At my age, I was not in their plans.

The next year, I signed with the Angels, but played only part of the season. My heart wasn't in it anymore after being in the big leagues. Going up was fine, but going down, no.

There's another thing. I played eleven years with good players alongside me. You're surrounded by good ball players in the majors who know how to play the game – play it right. I learned from good men: Marty Krug, Fred Haney and Bill McKechnie. You don't make mental errors. They would forgive you all the physical errors, but not the thinking errors. Then you go down and watch them day after day throwing games away. They pull so many rocks that it galls you. They pull so many skulls. It gets to you.

After the Angels in 1941, I went into the United States Navy (at San Diego) and finally got the chance to teach and coach young players. Later on, I became a minor league manager. My last job in baseball was as a scout for the New York Yankees, but my bargaining days with the likes of Fuchs, Quinn, Terry and Giles were over.

Author's Note:

During World War II, Wally served at the U. S. Naval Air Training Station in San Diego. He was discharged from the Navy after serving forty-three months, returning to baseball as a scout for the New York Yankees. Later, he managed minor league teams in Manchester, New Hampshire, Grand Fork, North Dakota and Twin Falls, Idaho. However, the lure of California drew Wally and Martha back to their home in Manhattan Beach, and he finally left organized baseball in 1950.

For the next thirteen years, Wally was employed by the Northrop Corporation, Aircraft Division. He moved on to the Northrop Institute of Technology where he was on the staff of the Aviation Technicians' School until his retirement ten years later.

In retirement, Wally became a familiar figure in his community. He was much in demand for speaking engagements and baseball ceremonials. He was also resident expert at morning seminars in Ron Wall's barbershop, and a long-time consultant during breakfast at the Kettle Restaurant. He is fondly remembered at both these important communication centers.

"That did it!"

NINE

BASEBALL AS WORK

A. Spring Training

The regular season started about the middle of April and closed about the first of October. The usual schedule in the major leagues was 154 games. In 1931, I played in 156 games because there were two ties. I don't think I missed an inning that year, and I think I played in all the exhibition games.

Spring training lasted about six weeks, beginning in February. The *Uniform Player's Contract* read: "The Club may require the Player to report for practice at such places as the Club may designate and to participate in such exhibition contests as may be arranged by the Club for a period of sixty days prior to the playing season..." The contract with the New York Giants stipulated a period of forty-five days.

In spring training we worked out about a week before we played exhibition games with teams in the area. We began with games between the Yanigans and the regulars.

Most ball players hate spring training, but I loved it. If you've been taking it easy, the first three days will kill you. When your legs are not ready, you get sore muscles, and then it takes another three days to get the soreness out. It's hard work.

Denny Carroll, the trainer for the San Francisco Seals, gave me advice on getting into shape – advice that I followed all through my playing days. It happened one winter in San Francisco when I got a real bad charley horse. I went to see Denny and he worked on it for me. That's when he gave me his program for getting into shape. He knew that I was going south to play with the Angels. This was his prescription:

"Wally, you go down to spring training two weeks ahead of time with pitchers and catchers. I want you to run for two weeks. Don't pick up the baseball. You go around the ball park. Keep going around the ball park, and when you get to home plate, sprint to first. Go around, hit home and sprint. And every day add a lap. As you run, keep moving your arms. After two weeks when the rest of the guys come in, your arm will come round. Your legs will be in shape, and your wind will be good. You won't have any trouble."

His advice proved to be sound, at least for me. "Remember," he said, "if you're in good condition, you won't get hurt as easy." The following season I played in 199 games, and I was never hurt except when I got beaned. I never pulled any muscles or anything else.

Even when I was a veteran ball player, I went to spring training ahead of time. I'd leave about the middle of February or sooner. If I was already signed up, I'd leave sooner. I went to Florida weighing 198 and I'd drop to 182 or thereabouts.

Before I went to spring training the first year with Boston, I got myself in pretty good shape. I was going to a big-league club from the minors, and I knew that the first impression was going to count. I had to battle for position with the other outfielders. I wanted to get a good start – and I did.

I hit one clear over the left-field fence into Tampa Bay, and right away the sports writers started picking it up from there. Also, I had a bit of advance publicity because I'd had a good season with the Angels in 1929. (Wally hit his first home run against the Yankees on March 22 as the Braves won, 11-2. Babe Ruth hit one for the Yankees in that same game.)

I just liked the game and I liked the exercise. I wish I could feel right now like I felt in those days. You feel good, you feel strong, you feel healthy. When I came into camp, I was thin, and a sports writer said, "Why don't you put on some weight so that you'll have something to lose when you come to spring training?"

I responded, "No, I'm getting off all the fat. When I pick up weight, it'll be muscle." I didn't have much fat anyway. so I enjoyed spring training. I enjoyed sweating. I enjoyed working out. I enjoyed being with the fellows and, of course, I enjoyed playing. Always.

You can see that they didn't have to tell me to take a couple of laps around the field. I knew that I had to get in shape and they didn't have to tell me how to do it. I believed in running – and I ran. In batting practice, you'd have a couple or three swings. On the last swing, I always ran around the bases. I'd sprint down to first (I don't see them doing that anymore). Then I'd trot around the bases, then go around the outfield. After that, I'd shag flies during batting practice.

Even though I was pretty good size, I was pretty fast. Bill

McKechnie used to have sprints, and I won nearly all the races. I lost very few in my time.

In Florida, all the teams training there were only a bus ride away, so we'd tour Florida. After the second week, they'd start weeding out. They'd send the guys they weren't going to use to minor-league clubs, their farm clubs, or cut them loose altogether.

The only time I didn't drive across the country to spring training in the majors was my first year, 1930. I was itching to get going, so I took the train to St. Petersburg, where the Braves held spring training. The Yankees were also training across town at another park. We had plenty of competition. The Cardinals were at Bradenton, the Dodgers at Clearwater, the Red Sox at Sarasota, Detroit at Lakeland and Washington was at Orlando. This was the famous "Grapefruit League."

The Braves stayed at the West Coast Inn. It was an old wooden two-story hotel built after the Civil War. It was a quaint place with creaking floors and the bathroom down the hall. It was convenient. We just walked across the street to Waterfront Park.

In those days, the Braves played the Yankees nine games every spring. Coming from the minors, I was really impressed. I was in awe of players like Babe Ruth and Lou Gehrig. We walked out in our dirty Braves uniforms and wrinkled caps. They came out in their nice, beautiful, clean pin-stripes. They were all precision. Their coach carried a couple of bags of balls. Everybody got one and they went to work just like the Army or something. The didn't even look at us or say, "Who the hell are we playing today?"

When Babe Ruth came up at batting practice, we were working on the sides. Everyone stopped what they were doing – everyone! The Babe would dump a few out of sight. After he was through hitting, we went back about our business, even though Lou Gehrig – also a great hitter – was coming up next.

The game hasn't changed much fundamentally in fifty years. If the manager puts you down on the card opening day as a result of your spring training, and you're out there in center field, the job is probably yours until someone takes it away from you. Once you're established, though, it's hard to unseat you – but you have to bear down all the time. However, once you have a reputation, you can go into a slump and they won't panic.

After you've played a while, say eight to ten years, you look down and see who's sitting on the bench – and remember that if you get out of line, that young guy looks pretty good. If he gets in and goes good, I might not get back into the lineup. So you bear down right to the end, right to the end of your career.

B. Exhibition Games and Other Annoyances

After we broke camp, we played exhibition games on our way north to Boston. We'd get off the train, play a game and move on. One year Washington went with us, and we played them all along the line. We wound up in Washington, D. C. – then we went ahead to Boston. Before the season opened in Boston, we would play a city series with the Red Sox, and a traditional game with Holy Cross College in Worcester.

In addition to the thirty or forty exhibition games played in spring training, there were many others during the regular season. Judge Fuchs was always building goodwill by scheduling games with local teams in the New England area. I can remember at least seventeen in one year at Boston on our "days off." We once even took the boat to Nova Scotia from Boston to play a game there.

The Judge liked that stuff; he wanted to be a good fellow. Some promoter over in Wollaston or Revere would say to him, "Hey, Judge, why don't you bring your team down and play our local team in a benefit game for the milk fund?"

He'd respond, "Yes, I can arrange that when we have an open date." Why not? It wasn't costing him anything but our days off. I do recall that we played one in Brockton, the shoe town, for the milk fund. It was a good cause, but it meant that we played eight games that week.

Sunday was a big day. There was a double-header every Sunday. They weren't scheduled. Nobody went to ball games on Mondays – these were depression times. Workers made sure they were on the job Mondays, so the owners took the old Monday games and moved them to Sundays. This left a lot of open dates, but the Judge would schedule exhibition games. He'd find someplace to take us. We even played on public playground parks around Boston.

The players didn't squawk too much about it. There was no union, and we felt we were lucky to be working, but we never looked forward to playing exhibition games. We got so damn tired of putting our uniforms on and taking them off. You got so tired that you didn't care, and then you could get hurt. Slide and break a leg, and for what?

Moreover, when you play some town team, you take winning for granted. Then about the sixth inning, we'd realize that those guys were beating us. We'd have to pick ourselves up off the floor. Sometimes it was too late.

A good example of what I mean was a game we played in Jamestown, New York. We were coming back from the West and it was an open date. We stopped off in a little town, Weston, New York, and met an electric train that bounced us all over hell on the way to Jamestown.

When the game started, lo and behold, out on the mound for Jamestown was this old-time big-league pitcher, Swede Erickson. I recognized him right away. When I was a kid, I had seen him pitch for the San Francisco Seals, and he won something like thirty games out there. Before that he had played for Detroit and Washington.

So we were playing this hometown team with a hometown umpire. Home plate itself was dug up about the batter's box. You couldn't stand close to the plate because of a sandy hole. On top of that this guy was cheating out there. He knew it and we knew it. He pitched spitters and that outside pitch all day long.

Out in center field I was sitting right off Lake Chatauqua. I had a bad back and I was miserable. They had us shut out with no hits and no runs for eight innings. I was muttering to myself, "This is embarrassing; when are we gonna get a hit off this guy?"

Finally we sent in a pinch hitter in the ninth. He bounced one someplace and got a scratch hit. Imagine a big league club playing semi-pros and getting beat one-to-nothing!

I could see us scheduling games occasionally with pretty good teams like Triple A – go down and play Indianapolis or Columbus or Newark. But I didn't like the idea of playing in motheaten ball parks that were all chewed up and with hard ground to play on. I was proud to be a big-league ball player. I didn't like to play under those conditions. It was humiliating.

When the All-Star Game came along, I thought we'd get those days off – the day before the game and the day after. But even then, some of the clubs would schedule exhibition games. When I was with the Reds, we went over to Dayton to play, instead of being able to have a few beers with the fellows, play a little golf and listen to the game on radio.

We also spent many days on the road traveling by train around the circuit. On our long trips where we played everybody there would be as many as 26 games. These were long trips – over three weeks. Some of the players used to ship their trunks in the baggage car, and would have them sent to the hotel. They would carry a little bag with their overnight stuff, but they'd save all their laundry until they got home. Then they would send it to the Chinese laundry; it was cheaper that way.

We got few days off from February when we arrived in camp to the last week of the season in early October. Connie Mack once suggested that there be a mid-season break to allow players to rest for a few days from the grind, but the idea was never adopted. No wonder we often prayed for rain!

When I was traded to the Giants in 1937, I first thought of going over the New Jersey to live. Apartments and houses were cheaper there, and probably nicer. But then I found out that I had to live in Manhattan – it was a club rule. Today they couldn't get away with that.

There was nothing stated specifically in the contract about where players had to live, but there was a catch-all clause: *The Player accepts as part of this contract the regulations printed on the third page hereof, and also such reasonable modifications as the Club may announce from time to time.* In other words, they just told you, and to my knowledge no one ever challenged this rule as unreasonable.

The reason that they wanted you to live in New York was to keep tabs on you. They could put the finger on you any time they wanted. The Giants also hired detectives to tail a player when they suspected him of having a little too much fun. For instance, they checked on Shanty Hogan, the catcher, who liked to make the rounds of the speakeasies in New York. The Giants, so far as I know, was the only club that did this.

If a player got caught violating any of the regulations, they could put him on the carpet: "You report to John McGraw." They could also use violations against him when it came time to discuss next year's contract.

Then, of course, they could always *"impose a reasonable fine and deduct the amount thereof from the Player's salary, or (may) suspend the Player without salary for a period not exceeding thirty days, or both, at the discretion of the Club." (REGULATION 6)*

The Giants also conducted a bed check when we were on the road. They didn't put you on your honor to be in your hotel room by midnight. I'm an early riser, so I was always in bed long before midnight, and I didn't like to be policed. I would go up to my room early with all kinds of reading material and lie in bed and read.

When I was sound asleep, they would come in to make sure it was me sleeping there – by turning on the light to wake me up. I had to leave the door unlocked until they checked. In the hotels that had transoms, they would then lock the door and throw the key in over the transom.

One time they did that and I couldn't get out in the morning. The key wouldn't work on my side of the door! I had to call a bellhop to get out. It was ridiculous and unnecessary.

C. On the Road

There were some club houses I didn't like, especially the one in Philadelphia. It looked like the dungeon in a Dumas story, with rats running around. The club house in center field was downstairs. It was dark and damp down there – and it had only two lousy showers. It wasn't clean. Even after you swept it out, it still looked dirty. You dressed nicely and then you got down there and hung up your clothes in a dusty locker.

Most of them were old club houses, but they were at least clean. Chicago had the best one at Wrigley Field. The Boston club house was big. A pot-bellied stove was our heat in the spring when it was ice-cold outside. That stove didn't heat the room completely, so we had to hang around it to keep warm.

Being on a club like the Boston Braves (God bless 'em, I don't like to knock them because it was depression days), you wouldn't take the best train. You got the second section, and they picked the Baltimore and Ohio from Philly to go to Pittsburgh. I didn't like that roadbed because it was kind of wobbly, with soft shoulders. Whatever it was, it made for a rough ride.

I didn't like the idea when you got into town and the ball park was far away. You were on your own to get there, and you paid your own way to the ball park. I didn't think it was fair. Usually, four or five guys jumped in a cab and split the bill. Today, they have a bus. Everyone hops into the bus and they go out in a body. This is the only way to do it. You keep everyone together.

Most of the time we had to take cabs. In Chicago, I walked. It was a pretty good walk – a couple of miles, I guess. In New York, we took the subway to play the Giants and the Dodgers, and that was all right.

The ball clubs usually stayed at the same hotel. In Pittsburgh, for instance, they all stayed at the Schenley Hotel, which was just a block and a half from the ball park. It was a good hotel, out of the downtown area of Pittsburgh. There was a park all around, Schenley Park, and there was a museum. They were also building the Cathedral of Learning at the University of Pittsburgh.

In fact, the Schenley was a family hotel. A lot of older retired women lived there, widows, and people with money. You got a lot of service there, and after prohibition they had a tap room downstairs and a big veranda which was nice on a summer evening. Everyone just sat out there and talked. There was nothing else to do unless you wanted to go into downtown Pittsburgh – and no one bothered to do that. I went into downtown Pittsburgh once in eleven years (I didn't even know what downtown looked like!) with some other players to see a burlesque show.

Some hotels were not to my liking. I'll never forget one time we were staying in downtown Chicago, at the Congress, I think, and road secretary Duffy Lewis (once a member of that great outfield of Lewis, Speaker and Hooper), asked me to take a walk with him to look over the Edgewater Beach to see if the club should change hotels. Duffy liked class, see. We went to the Edgewater Beach, which was right on the lake. It was a better hotel.

Duffy talked to the manager and apparently made some kind of a deal with him. I guess Duffy wanted to get back to Boston and talk it over with Judge Fuchs about making the move to the Edgewater Beach, which was closer to the ball park, too. We did make the change. I liked the atmosphere there. They had nice rooms, and they put either a bowl of fruit or some flowers in every room. When you left a call with the operator, she would call and tell you the outdoor air temperature, the speed and direction of the wind and how to dress. I got a kick out of that. This was big-league stuff!

When I was with the Braves, we stayed at the Alamac Hotel in New York at 72nd and Broadway. Then we moved to the Victoria, down closer to Times Square. The Alamac, as far as the rooms were concerned, was all right, but the food was terrible. The players squawked and squawked about it. I remember once when Earl Sheely was pouring a cup of tea out of one of those little teapots, and a piece of fish came out of the nozzle. That did it! He went to our manager and said, "You ain't gonna put us up in this hotel. I got a dirty teapot with a piece of fish coming out. I'm gonna rent my own room someplace." We got out of the Alamac on account of that.

Earl was a great big man, six feet, three-and-one-half-inches tall. He was blonde with curly hair; a nice-looking man with a good physique. He was a good first baseman, but he couldn't run. He had played with the White Sox. I played against him in the Coast League when he played for Sacramento. He was very good on low throws, and he used to tell the shortstop to throw the ball in the dirt to make him look good. He was a pretty good hitter.

I stole 13 bases that year because Earl could hit and run. I'd start and they'd pitch out, or whatever, and I'd steal a base. McKechnie didn't usually go for a hit and run, but with Earl he would – because he'd get a piece of the ball all the time. He would protect you by throwing the bat at the ball, or he'd foul it off.

Ball players all like to eat. I haven't seen one who didn't have a hearty meal two or three times a day. A lot of them skipped lunch or had a very light lunch. We played day ball and didn't want to get overloaded with food. I never did. Maybe a glass of milk and a small piece of apple pie would be my limit for lunch. We all liked Boston because it had good sea food. Boston was a good town for eating. And we all liked the Schenley Hotel in Pittsburgh because in those days they had chefs in hotels, and you really got some great meals.

After the game we'd have two or three beers. It tasted good whether it was home brew or beer imported from Canada. Now we were relaxed after the game; dinner would be a little late. On account of the ball game we would eat, say, around seven in the evening. The we could tear into a steak, baked potato, lettuce-and-tomato salad, shrimp cocktail and wind up with a parfait and a pot of coffee. I used to order not by the menu but from memory. I never looked at the right-hand side of a menu at the price, because we signed for the check. You could probably get by on four bucks a day. Can you imagine that? Four bucks a day! I would just about make it because of my breakfast and dinner. The Giants didn't have any limit. You could eat all you wanted and just sign the check.

There are twenty-five guys on a club, and you don't see eye-to-eye with everyone, but you gotta be friendly. You are living with them for six months, but when the game is over, you go your way and they go theirs. Sometimes there were some guys in the club that we didn't like – a pop-off guy or maybe the clubhouse lawyer – the guy who was undermining the manager, always talking against the club and knocking somebody. The average player just wants to get out there, play the game, get his paycheck, go home and not worry.

Every team got a clown, and it's good to have a clown. He keeps you laughing and loose. Rabbit Maranville was the clown in Boston. And then we had a guy like Shanty Hogan, a big, good-natured Irishman, weighing 275 pounds. He laughed and said funny things. There was all that stuff going on in the club. Usually you got along; generally ball players are pretty good guys.

D. In the Ball Parks

In attempting to make judgements on players, there are so many situations and conditions that statistics in record books and encyclopedias can't show. There are so many things to take into account when comparing the performances of teams and players in different times and places. I mention many of them throughout this book. However, these additional explanations and illustrations of the differences in parks during the Thirties – may make my point clearer.

The conditions of the park in which you played were very important, and especially in your home park where you played half your games. The most obvious difference was the physical size of the parks. Every park in the National League in my time had different dimensions. Right field down the line at the Polo Grounds was 257 feet, just seven feet over the minimum permitted. Right field down the line at Crosley Field in Cincinnati was 377. Right field down the line in Philadelphia was 280 feet; in Boston it was 364 feet. In Pittsburgh, the right field line was 300 feet; the left field line, 385 feet.

Not only was there this great variation in size, but clubs would sometimes tailor their parks to suit their current players. They would move fences in and out, and raise or lower them, to accommodate their hitters.

A good illustration of what these different dimensions meant can be seen in the home run production in various parks. In 1935, the most home runs were hit at the Polo Grounds in New York (150), and at Baker Bowl in Philadelphia (120). The least home runs were hit in Cincinnati (36), and at Pittsburgh (57). The Giants hit 84 home runs in their home park, but only 39 on the road. On the other hand, the Cincinnati team hit only 18 at home, but they hit 55 on the road. Some difference!

At my home park, Braves Field, the home run total was 75; we hit 34 and the visitors hit 41. The preceding year, 1934, the total at Boston was 63, while at New York it was 118.

If you look in the record book for the Twenties and Thirties, you will notice that Pittsburgh led the league most often in triples. The main reason was that Forbes Field was a "triples park;" it was big and fast. Balls hit in the alleys were usually triples. You couldn't cut across and intercept the ball. Outfielders would have to head for the fence, get it off the fence and throw it.

Paul Waner, the great Pittsburgh outfielder, hit 190 triples in his career, and Pie Traynor, Pittsburgh manager and Hall of Fame third baseman, hit 164. The only time that Kiki Cuyler led the league in triples was when he played in Pittsburgh.

Braves Field was not conducive to triples. It had a slow outfield. They let the grass grow a little high, and the prevailing east wind blew in from right field. I played center field there. Sometimes I'd be playing in left center, and a guy would belt one into right center. Ordinarily, that should be a triple up the alley to the fence, but I'd go after that ball and would be able to catch up with it and grab it. What looked at first like an easy double or triple just laid up there for me to catch.

When I did this, I'd look at the hitter who was just about ready to round second base. He'd turn around and look at me as if to say in disgust, "You know what you can do with this ball park!" Also, we sometimes played in temperatures as low as thirty-eight degrees, which never pleased our visitors, either.

A good contrast in parks would be Braves Field in Boston and Baker Bowl in Philadelphia. Boston was spacious, and was known as a "pitcher's park." Philadelphia, on the other hand, was known as a "band box" for its small size, and was considered a "hitter's park."

Baker Bowl was an all-wooden structure that held about 16,000 spectators, but they seldom filled it. That little park was a hitter's delight. The visiting club would come in there and look at that right field – and all of a sudden they felt big and strong.

The pitchers were shell-shocked in that park. You had a fence 285 feet away, and even though it was forty feet high, it scared a pitcher to death. Baker Bowl was a paradise for Chuck Klein and other sluggers who called it home. Klein would sit on top of that plate and he'd pull the outside ball against the wall. He was a hard out in that park. He tattooed the wall because he had a target to shoot at. You just got half a hold of it and you could hit the fence. In addition to his home run production, Klein hit lots of doubles: 59 in 1930 and 50 in 1932.

I don't mean to put Klein down, because he really was a good hitter. He hit the ball on the line and leveled on them. But that short right field led to inflated statistics – not just in hitting, but in fielding as well. In 1930, the Philadelphia outfield had 68 assists, of which Chuck Klein in right field got 44, about four times as many as the average. In contrast, the whole Braves outfield had a total of 33; Brooklyn had 31 and Pittsburgh had 34.

Naturally, scores were high in Philadelphia, and Philadelphia pitchers as a group had an earned run average of 6.71, compared to 4.03 for Brooklyn and 4.97 for the League. In the first ten games at Philadelphia in 1930, it was the Phillies, 73 runs; visitors, 83 runs. They beat Brooklyn in the second game, 16-15; in the ninth game, Brooklyn beat them 16-9. On July 23, it was Pittsburgh 16 and the Phils 15. On July 24, Chicago beat them 19-15.

In Philadelphia there was another difference that was sometimes significant. The spectators sat only about 15 to 20 feet behind the catcher. There was no foul territory to speak of. In other parks it was at least sixty feet, and at Forbes Field it was ninety feet. Lots of room to catch foul balls, but also you could sometimes score from second on a passed ball. I should mention something favorable about Baker Bowl. The playing field itself was good.

Up north in Boston, the visitors responded differently. It was a long right field – and home run hitters batting on the right side didn't hit in Braves Field. In fact, some of them became sick when they got to Boston. They looked at that big ball park and saw the wind blowing, and they didn't feel good. They didn't want to get in there.

Every park had something odd or different. The Polo Grounds was high in home run production. It was short on the line, but the park swung out and away. It got very deep, and really wasn't an easy park to hit in. You'd get a cheap home run, and then you'd get one taken away from you.

The playing field was good in New York. There was a little slope behind the infield. The outfielders bunched, positioning themselves to take away hits. The ball would carom off the concrete wall, and you had to learn to play the angle shot. Mel Ott, who played his entire career there, became very good at doing that. In one season he had 26 assists in right field.

In 1930, the left field in Cincinnati was way out. I was the fourth guy ever to clear the fence. Later they shortened it, but it was still fifty feet farther down the line than in most parks today. There was a gradual slope up to the outfield fence. Before a game I would practice shagging flies to get accustomed to balls bouncing off the fence. Cincinnati was also the hottest park in the summer. It was below street level, and one time the thermometer registered 119 degrees in the dugout. The milkshake drinkers would pass out, but the beer drinkers would be O. K!

When I first went into Ebbets Field in Brooklyn, it was a big park in center and left, with a short right field. A little later, they built double-deck stands, shortening the field and making it a hitter's park. They also put a screen on top of the concrete wall in right field.

Wrigley Field in Chicago was always kept in good condition. The wind blowing in off the lake would hold up fly balls. There was ivy on the wall, and it's still there. If the ball caught in the ivy, it was a ground-rule double. At first there were no bleachers, but later they put them in right and center field. The white shirts in warm weather would make it difficult for the batter to follow the ball, particularly if the pitcher had a side-arm delivery.

Sportsman's Park in St. Louis was fast and hard. The St. Louis Browns played there, too, so the park was used all the time. It was good for hitters, but tough for the fielders. You had to play bad hops in the outfield. Right field was a tough sun field because the hitter was in the shadow. There was a double-deck from the left field to the right field foul line. In front of the right field bleachers was a screen, and the ball was considered to be in play if it hit that screen. Here, too, the white shirts in center field were hard on the batter.

These few examples make it obvious, I think, that the conditions of the home park often have a strong influence on statistics, both for hitting and fielding. Therefore, an evaluation of the performance of players, in order to be fair, must take into account these sharp differences.

131

"Thanks for the memories, Wally!"

TEN

A SERIOUSLY MEANT
UNIVERSE OF ITS OWN

A. The Paying Critics – The Fans

As Wally and I were writing about the Braves, we wondered if there were still any fans left in the Boston area who remembered Wally and the Braves of the Thirties. In May, 1981, we sent a letter to the Sports Editor of the *Boston Globe*, telling readers that we were writing a book about that era and asking them to send us their recollections.

> Former Boston Braves' outfielder Wally Berger – a favorite here in the '30s – has asked for help in writing a book. His letter:
>
> "With the help of George Snyder, a history teacher, I am writing a book about baseball in the '20s and '30s, and especially the years when I played with the Boston Braves (1930-37).
>
> "I would like to hear from readers of The Globe who remember those times and would send their recollections to me. I will acknowledge all responses promptly and will give credit for any that I include in our book My address is:
>
> Wally Berger
> 124 21st Street
> Manhattan Beach, Calif. 90266
> *(May 5, 1981)*

Within a few days we got our answer. Wally was relaxing at home in the evening when he got a call from Boston. Two old-time fans getting happy in a bar decided to telephone Wally in Manhattan Beach. They told him that they had seen his letter in the *Globe*, and they reminisced until their telephone money ran out.

133

During the next month, we received letters, calls and packages from over sixty fans. They sent books, pictures, cartoons, drawings, clippings and memories. At least two letters were seven pages long.

Among the respondents was Abraham Alpert, who had been bat boy and clubhouse boy for the Braves. Leo Liston sent a photocopy of his membership in the Knot Hole Gang. William McFarland identified himself as a "car jockey" during the depression and said that he had driven Wally and his wife many times. Robert Jordan said that he sold newspapers and sundries outside Braves Park. Fred Cusick, one of a number of Knot Hole Gang members who wrote, became a sports announcer and now does Bruins' hockey games on WSBK-TV. He wrote an interesting account of his experiences, including a memoir of Fred Hoey, who announced games on radio.

The oldest fan was Stanley Smith, Captain of the Yale basketball team of 1914. He included a copy of an article which featured him and Nat Holman, the famous basketball star.

Harriet Nemiccolo was the only woman to respond. Now a librarian at the School of Social Work at Boston College, she became a Wally Berger fan in 1932, at the age of ten. We have corresponded frequently with her since 1981. She has become a most helpful consultant and supporter. We asked her to write about Ladies' Day, and her article is included. Thanks, Harriet.

In Boston, we got the big crowds on the weekends. We'd get our out-of-towners. They'd come down from Maine, Vermont, New Hampshire and over from Rhode Island. These were the fans who would give you hell. They'd read about you all week – you did this and you did that. Then when they came to see you, you had to live up to their expectations. If you had a bad day, they would boo or tease you.

In 1935, when the Braves won only 38 games all season, I can't remember that the fans got on us too badly. And in Chicago one season when Kiki Cuyler got in a slump, and went something like 0-25, the fans cheered him when he came to bat. They tried to encourage him to get a hit and break the spell.

Boston was a great sporting town and Boston fans as a whole were great. So were the Chicago fans. They were the two best in the League.

Sometimes the behavior of the fans did bother the players. There was always a sprinkling of rowdies, sometimes more than a sprinkling. However, I had been baptized in the minor leagues.

Occasionally a couple of leather-lungs sitting behind me would start to irritate me. If you let on that you heard the razzing and abuse, they would taunt you with the cry of "rabbit ears." Your would hear: "Hey, rabbit – hey, you got rabbit ears!"

In the outfield I played about 25 or 30 feet from the fence. The hecklers behind me in the bleachers were only forty feet away – that's close. Unless there was a big crowd, you could hear every damn thing in the stadium. With thirty or forty thousand all you heard was a big hum – just mumble, mumble, mumble. And you concentrate – you shut everything out of your mind.

The other extreme was a weekday afternoon in Cincinnati. The Braves and the Reds were both down at the bottom, and we had only about 150-200 spectators. In a park that seated 30,000, you could hardly see them. All we heard then was the guy selling hot dogs – or that one loudmouth.

Generally, my policy with hecklers was to act as if I didn't hear them. If you ignored them, they finally got tired and gave up. If you turned around and said something, they had a lot of fun. Once I got mad at a couple of young fellows and turned around a little bit. Then they really let me have it. They hollered out things that weren't true: "Berger, we saw you drunk last night in McGurk's Tavern," or something like that. They could get pretty nasty.

I usually thought that it was their prerogative. They paid to get in, and that's what paid my salary. If they come out to boo, let them boo. They'll cheer on another day.

Brooklyn, especially, was that way from inning to inning. Babe Herman once got hit in the head with a fly ball and they booed him at length. Then he hit a home run and they were all for him.

Not always, though. I saw Herman get booed in Brooklyn when he hit a home run. He had been up a couple of times with men on and didn't deliver. He belted one with nobody on and the crowd booed him as if to say, "Why did you hit it now? Why didn't you hit it with somebody on base?" That didn't bother Herman. He never was a real good outfielder. He played some easy outs into doubles and triples, and he sometimes passed runners on bases, but that seemed to happen in Brooklyn. They did those things – I don't know why.

Once in a while a heckler would stir up a player and the player would go up into the stands after him. In the Coast League I saw a big pitcher named Tomlin do that. A heckler kept on him. After three or four innings, Tomlin couldn't take it any more. He chased the guy right out of the ball park!

Some hecklers would pick a favorite target and never let up. At the Polo Grounds there was some fan on Mel Ott for a long time. He sat in the center field bleachers right near the clubhouse, and every time Mel would walk to the plate, this fan would shout, "pop fly!" If Mel did pop up, which he didn't do very often, the heckler would really rub it in.

Finally it got to Ott. One afternoon he was really burned up. He said to a police sergeant who used to come into the clubhouse after the games, "I'm going to go get that son-of-a-bitch." The cop, a friendly Irishman with a brogue, calmed Mel down saying, "No you won't, Mr. Ott. You don't want to do that. He'd have you down in court suing you for assault and battery and all that."

From the clubhouse to the dugout at Brooklyn, there was a walk under the stands enclosed with a wire-mesh fence. As the visiting team – the enemy – walked through, the fans on either side would give you the business. We felt like animals in a zoo.

When we ran to the clubhouse in Philadelphia, we always had to take off our caps – otherwise the fans would snatch the caps off our heads as we passed between the bleachers, and run off with them. They thought it was great sport. Also, they always seemed to have a couple of hucksters – one sat at third base, and the other one at first. Between the two, they really let the visiting team have it.

Brooklyn had a woman in the upper deck right over home plate. She got on you the moment you walked onto the field. I think they must have given her a season pass just to sit up there and agitate the visiting club. She got pretty dirty. She'd dig up things on you either from the papers or hearsay, or just make them up. Rabbit Maranville squelched her for a short time one afternoon. He walked out, paused, and looked up. Then he said, "My God, Mary, who hit you with the ax?"

Cincinnati fans thought a good ball game was Cincinnati, 18 runs; visitors, nothing. If you lost one-to-nothing in twenty innings, you were a bunch of bums. In July, 1939, we were thirteen games ahead, and had a winning streak of at least ten games. One of the poorer teams in the League came to town and beat us something like ten-to-two. We got razzed unmercifully. I thought, "What the hell do they want? We're way out front, we were on a long winning streak. If we're going to get beat, we might as well get beat bad. There were no post-mortems on a game like that. You just got whipped. You take it, that's all."

In all the years I played ball – World Series, All-Star Games, tight pennant races – I don't think there was anything like a New York Giants-Brooklyn Dodgers game. I played with the Giants just after the time Bill Terry was asked by reporters about the Brooklyn team and he answered, "Brooklyn? Are they still in the league?" Nothing could have infuriated the Brooklyn fans more.

When we played Brooklyn, I took the subway to the park. Kids met you in front of the subway exit, followed you all the way to the entrance and pressed around you for autographs. The streets were barricaded with mounted policemen on guard and nobody got through without identification. Once they wouldn't let me through and I had to get someone to vouch for me.

The game was sold out and filled up by noontime, although it didn't start until three. One time Mel Ott and I started up the stairs to the dugout. I said, "Go ahead, Mel." He said, "No, you go ahead." So I preceded him up the stairs, and as soon as the fans saw me in a Giants' uniform, the boos started and continued in one loud roar. I was dumbfounded. They gave us the raspberry even before the game started – before anything happened!

The fans in Brooklyn would bring in grocery bags full of "food." After all, it was a long wait, but a lot of the "food" consisted of rotten apples, tomatoes and empty beer bottles--ammunition to fire at the hated Giants. When an argument started down at home plate, I'd move out of range. I knew what was going to happen: here comes the barrage!

Hank Lieber was playing in center field one day and a guy with a good arm hit him square in the back of the head with a ripe apple that splattered all over him. We all marched infield about thirty feet to get out of range of the throwers in the upper deck. When they called time, it took about fifteen minutes to clean the garbage off the field.

Another time, Dick Bartell, leading off the inning, bitched about a called strike. That was the signal to throw things. Out came the bottles; they were flying all around him, but he stayed out there at home plate. Somebody said, "Dick has a lot of guts to stand up to that kind of treatment."

Not me, I thought he should have taken cover. We had no protection, not even the plastic helmets the batters wear today. Even a helmet wouldn't help much if a bottle hit you in the head. I think security is tighter today on what you can bring into the stadium, and beverages are all served in paper cups.

B. The Boston Fans Respond

Abraham Alpert
Swampscott, Massachusetts

Richard Botsch
Falmouth, Massachusetts

Bob Brady
Braintree, Massachusetts

Robert E. Bumpus
Cambridge, Massachusetts

Frank X. Burns
Somerville, Massachusetts

Richard M. Cochrane
West Springfield, Massachusetts

Burton E. Clark
Sutton, Massachusetts

Ed Conley
Randolph, Massachusetts

Tom Tucker Conlon
Tewksbury, Massachusetts

Harold Corvini
Plymouth, Massachusetts

Fred M. W. Cusick
Cape Cod, Massachusetts

Richard Dansghow
Chicopoo, Massachusetts

Thomas Doherty
Westborough, Massachusetts

James L. Ferullo
Brighton, Massachusetts

James W. Haley
North Easton, Massachusetts

Charles B. Holland
Quincy, Massachusetts

Leo P. Horne, Sr.
East Boston, Massachusetts

Barney Huxley
Brighton, Massachusetts

Wells M. Johnson
Lynnfield, Massachusetts

Robert G. Jordan
Cambridge, Massachusetts

James F. Kelley
North Quincy, Massachusetts

Warren N. Kellogg
Exeter, New Hampshire

Stuart M. King
Millis, Massachusetts

Arthur J. Lewis
Brookline, Massachusetts

Robert E. Lewis
Brewster, Massachusetts

Leo M. Liston
Everett, Massachusetts

Frank Mandosa
Roslindale, Massachusetts

Raymond Mangion
Reading, Massachusetts

Andrew T. Manley
Melrose, Massachusetts

C. J. Matheson
Burlington, Massachusetts

William A. McFarland
Cambridge, Massachusetts

Justin A. McKean
Natick, Massachusetts

Stewart C. McLeish
Everett, Massachusetts

Nando "Andy" M. Melchiorri
North Attleboro, Massachusetts

Peter T. Miller
Foxboro, Massachusetts

Ernest Morse
Beverly, Massachusetts

Al Mosca
East Boston, Massachusetts

Harriet Nemiccolo
Auburndale, Massachusetts

Thomas J. O'Connor
Springfield, Massachusetts

Leo T. O'Keefe
West Roxbury, Massachusetts

Sumner Peck
Whitefield, New Hampshire

Alec Poule
Duxbury, Massachusetts

John Quigley	Laurence J. Stange
Springfield, Massachusetts	South Deerfield, Massachusetts
E. Arthur Renzetti	Harold S. Stewart
Canton, Massachusetts	Hyannis, Massachusetts
Harold F. Riley	John H. Sullivan
Newburyport, Massachusetts	Malden, Massachusetts
Sol Rogers	Hrach Vahe
Walpole, Massachusetts	Watertown, Massachusetts
Stanley K. Smith	John C. Weilandt
Longmeadow, Massachusetts	Belmont, Massachusetts
Paul Stafford	William Winterbottom
Southbridge, Massachusetts	Philadelphia, Pennsylvania

C. Ladies' Day in Boston *(By Harriet Tirrell Nemiccolo)*

For many women who grew up in the Boston area during the depression thirties, Ladies' Day was their only chance to see their beloved Braves or Red Sox in action. They simply could not afford regular admission prices.

At first, Friday was Ladies' Day. Women were admitted to the ball game as guests of the management, either at Braves Field or Fenway Park, depending upon which team was in town. They paid only a ten-cent federal tax.

In 1933, Judge Fuchs of the Braves and Bob Quinn of the Red Sox jointly changed Ladies' Day to Saturday. This was very welcome news to women fans, as well as being a generous gesture on the part of the owners, since Saturday was the best attendance day of the week. (Sunday baseball was not played by professional teams at this time in Boston.)

It is not surprising that the Boston clubs made these overtures to women. Bob Quinn had established a very successful Ladies' Day as early as 1907, when he managed a minor-league club in Columbus, Ohio. And Bill McKechnie, the Braves manager, was warm in his response to women fans. The women, in turn, loved McKechnie and admired his quiet but firm leadership. Besides, the women were more encouraging to the individual players than the more demanding male fans.

Official baseball records do not include the origin and history of Ladies' Day, nor is the term indexed in the *Encyclopedia of Baseball*. It has been recorded in a few newspaper and magazine articles written mostly by women, none of whom were baseball writers.

Our interest here is centered on Ladies' Day during the Thirties and early Forties. During this period, many women were drawn to baseball because it was the All-American game. Our brothers played the game almost every summer day. The radio broadcasts could be heard at home, often in competition with the lawn mower. Everywhere we went, someone was listening to the game. It was the ubiquitous sound of summer.

Because it is not officially documented, Ladies' Day recollections are largely personal. For me the frame of reference is Braves Field, now Boston University's Nickerson Field. The building resembled a giant stucco stable house with gable-like gate entrances. Inside, practically everything was made of wood and painted dark green. The press box, hanging precariously from the grandstand, seemed encased in a wooden frame. There was a section of the bleachers in right field, shaped like a jury box, for which it was aptly named. The grandstand seats were painted green slats and were very comfortable.

Most folks arrived at the park by trolley car. Many others walked. Those who drove could park right on Granby Street at the entrance. It was always exciting to approach the gates and hear the hawkers call out, "Get your scorecard here!" Once inside, it was such a pleasure to watch batting practice and size up the visiting team. The scene was tranquil, despite all the activity. Best of all, when the game was over, we could run onto the field, possibly get an autograph, shake hands with a player, or even run the bases.

Women became very involved in the game. They would spot a player striding from the bull pen or coming out of the dugout and announce his name to all within earshot before it came over the loudspeaker. With their knowledge of records, line-ups and batting orders, many would have made good statisticians. Some that I knew missed many a good play while meticulously marking the scorecard. They loved quoting the record books and choosing the All-Star teams. Most of all, they were totally devoted to their team and their favorite players. Nothing was more poignant to the female fan than to see a player, applauded for a great play, return to the dugout, lift his cap and smile at the stands.

In 1931, my friend, Agnes Maytum of Cambridge, accompanying her father, went to Braves Field for the first time. The game was a graduation present for her completion of junior high school. She never stopped following the Braves until they moved to Milwaukee in 1953.

In 1932 I saw the Braves for the first time. I remember that Pepper Martin hit a home run for the St. Louis Cardinals to defeat the home team. On that day I fell in love with baseball, and Wally Berger became my first and best baseball hero. Because of male teasing, I had to defend him a lot. Although I never met him, he always impressed me as a hard-working, modest, gentlemanly player.

Bill Veeck, maverick owner of the Cleveland Indians, built a new stadium in the mid-forties. He immediately established Ladies' Day on Saturday with this announcement: "Women are people just like everyone else, and American people love baseball. All a lady needs is a proper introduction."

Back in 1931 and 1932, Agnes Maytum and I received that proper introduction. We attended our first games with our fathers, Daniel Maytum and John Tirrell.

Thanks for the memories, Wally!

D. The Professional Critics

In Los Angeles I knew a number of sportswriters: Braven Dyer, Martin Burke, Bobby Ray, Matt Gallager, Sid Ziff, Johnny Old, Bob Hunter and Mark Kelly. They were all a little different about reporting a game. They emphasized different aspects.

Some really gave you the business. When I lost a ball in the sun and it hit me on the head, Martin Burke said: "It is positively dangerous to pasture big Berger in the sun field. He's a nice prospect and there is no sense in having him killed" And a big headline over the story of the game read: BERGER CATCHES ONE FLY – ON HIS FOREHEAD.

Another one said of me, "He can't field, can't hit, but he throws good." In my judgement, my throwing, though adequate, was the least impressive of my skills.

The only reporter who became a friend of mine was Bobby Ray. This was unusual because reporters usually keep their distance so that they can write fairly. But Bobby lived in my neighborhood in Los Angeles and we got to know each other pretty well. He sometimes covered high school football games and I would go along to spot for him. He had a column called *The X-Ray*. At another time he called it *Pick-Ups*.

Mark Kelly, I remember, couldn't say a nice thing about anyone. He panned the club all the time, and at one time or another had most of the players upset at what he wrote about them. He never came around to talk with the players.

Once he picked on Slug Tolson, a good hitter who had come down from the Cubs. Tolson's power was to right center; he used to hit them into those bleachers in right center at old Wrigley Field. Kelly criticized him for that, saying, "When is Tolson going to hit a ball into left field?" I thought it was ridiculous. Who cares if it goes over the fence in right field, left field, or center?

One afternoon Slug hit two over the left field fence. As he rounded third, he thumbed his nose at Kelly and shouted to him: "There's your left field fence. Write that one up!"

You didn't see the sportswriters too much in the minor leagues like Los Angeles. They didn't come to the clubhouse too often. If you had an exceptional day, someone would come down and talk to you about it, but they got all the information out of the ball players during spring training. They'd get their background then and the rest of the time you didn't see them much. If you went to any of the doings, maybe you'd run into a few.

In Boston, the chief baseball writer on the *Globe* was Jim O'Leary, an oldtimer. He had been a telegrapher at one time, and was supposed to be the one who sent the word around the world that the Battleship *Maine* had blown up in Havana harbor – just before the United States declared war on Spain in 1898.

O'Leary was a character. He was heavy-set, wore a big engineer's cap over his white hair, and always had a big cigar in his mouth. He liked ball players and never seemed to knock them. It seemed to me that he always tried to write something good about you, and if you had a bad day, he just didn't say too much. He would report a bad play, but he never dwelt on it. Uncle Jim liked me and wrote me up all the time.

On the other hand, Paul Shannon of the *Post* – these were all Irishmen from Boston – was more on the critical side. He would pick you to pieces if you went bad. Shannon didn't particularly like me. He and O'Leary were always needling each other. They were always feuding.

Of course, when I went to St. Petersburg, I met all the sportswriters covering baseball down there. They stayed in the same hotel, so they were around the lobby and in the clubhouse and out at the ball park. You'd talk to them all the time.

All the stuff they saw in Florida, they sent back to the Boston papers. It got the fans all excited about the club. Newcomers were "built up" a little bit so that when the team began its season in Boston, they came out to see you. They've been writing about you down in spring training – especially if you hit a few home runs or something.

Other writers in Boston were Burt Whitman, Joe Cashman and Johnny Drohan. We all liked Drohan, who was a fine storyteller. On the train, we'd sit in the club car and listen to him. He kept us entertained with his clever use of dialect.

Sometimes I wasn't even thinking about getting a writeup and I'd pick up the paper and say, "My God, did I say that?" They'd give us pretty good coverage in the spring, and of course you had the good days – when you got a good writeup.

When they'd write up the game and they wanted something on the side, they'd come into the clubhouse and interview the players. Say a guy is hitting in fifteen straight games or something--they'll come down and talk about that. Sometimes they got into your personal life, asking questions about your marriage or what you do for entertainment and relaxation.

One of the most surprising interviews that stuck in my mind was the one I had with Franky Graham of the *New York Times*. I didn't even know that it was an interview at the time. We were sitting in the train, just talking. He asked me a lot of questions like where I was born, what I did in San Francisco, and how I got started in baseball.

Graham didn't take a note, just sat there without pencil or paper. I though we were just having a bull session. The next day, someone told me about the article. It was almost word-for-word what I had told him, and it was a pretty good-sized article, too. I chuckled at myself for not knowing he was interviewing me, and wondered how he could remember all those things.

Most sportswriters seemed to have their favorites. I read the papers every day whether the baseball news was good or bad; I took the bitter with the sweet. I figured that if you played badly, you deserved to be panned. That was the writers' job. We were paid to play major-league quality, and the fans came out to see that kind of baseball.

Also, I wanted to see what they said about me, even if it was bad. When it was bad, I saved those clippings, too, with the thought in mind that I'd make them eat those words someday.

Ball players were affected by what the papers said about them. They could stir you up a bit, particularly if they wrote something that you don't think you warranted, a knock of some kind. Maybe you didn't think you should have received that blast, but you have to take that, too, because you like it when they build you up.

On the road, when you were winning, you might get three or four writers who would go along, but if you're going real bad, you didn't see a sportswriter on the trip. They would take the United Press box score off the wire and that would be it.

So far as radio was concerned, I was a little shy of it. I was afraid I would make a mistake and be laughed at. I didn't like to go to banquets for the same reason. Generally, I turned down most invitations.

In Cincinnati, Red Barber was always asking me to come up there after a game, but I didn't want to go. I avoided it if I could. In Boston, I seldom went on radio unless it was with a group of players.

Once I was interviewed in San Francisco in my second year with the Angels. The club had just changed managers. A sportscaster wanted my views on Marty Krug who was leaving, and Jack Lellivelt who was coming in. This was in 1929. Right away he asked me who I liked best as manager. I was fond of Marty, and Jack was a really nice guy, so I didn't have to play any favorites. I felt it coming. I said they were both good managers, but that they used different techniques. I wasn't going to let them put me on a spot.

I was glad I went to that interview because I got to meet Max Schmeling, who was then just starting out as a fighter in America. He looked so much like Jack Dempsey that I had to stare. He turned out to be a pretty good fighter!

I really didn't think of the box office. I played because I liked to play, and I played to win. Babe Ruth had all the color, and if you were a ball player in New York, you got all the publicity in the world. All the wire services and a number of important publications were there.

For most of my major-league career, I was way up there in Boston, so if I was famous anywhere, it was mainly in New England.

E. Managers as Leaders

The most important aspect of managing is handling men. You have twenty-five men on a club, all with different personalities. You're with them for six to eight months including spring training. It's the use of psychology. You have to keep them happy, but you also have to be firm. You've got to be fair, and you've got to be consistent. Most of all, you must have their respect.

They don't have to yell and scream out there. The players are men, not kids. If you have a bulldog manager, a mean son-of-a-bitch like Ivan "the Terrible" Olson who was half-mad all the time, you play hard because you're half-mad, too. You might even play a little extra, be an extra step faster when you're a little angry. But if you have a Bill McKechnie or a Connie Mack, you'll break your leg for them. They were leaders. You liked them, you respected them and you wanted their approval. Either method will obviously achieve results. (I played for both types of managers, McKechnie in Boston and Cincinnati, and Olson in Pocatello.)

Some managers may be poor psychologists, and they may not be good at public relations, but they all know how to play the game in the major leagues. They can evaluate players. They know strategy – when to pull a pitcher, when to sacrifice, steal, or hit-and-run. They play different systems and have different styles. Often it depends on the kind of players they have, the park they are playing in and the conditions under which they are playing.

We usually had meetings at the start of a series, especially at the beginning of the year. For example, our first game might have been with the Giants, so we'd go through the hitters, talking over what we knew about them and what to watch out for. We might not have another meeting, or there might be a meeting just for the pitchers who are scheduled to pitch.

The manager got up there in his jock strap and put his one foot on the chair and sat and talked over the hitters, and some guy would raise his hand. He wanted to comment, and then they would get to talking about that. Maybe the manager didn't go for what this fellow suggested, so it would wind up most of the time that you did what the manager "asked" you to do. Sometimes he would agree to a different opinion: "Try it. If you think you can get the opposing guy out with this certain pitch, O. K., try it." But if it boomerangs – too bad.

An example of a situation where they'd call a special meeting would be breaking training. Maybe a few of the boys went out on the town and got themselves a few too many drinks and it got back to the manager. He would call a meeting on that to remind them again about the rules. "You have to be in your room by midnight, and we don't want anyone drinking any hard liquor." He wouldn't mention any names.

He would say, "There's been a few boys in this club who broke training. I don't like you to take this thing second-handed. These people call me up, you know, and tell me they saw you in the bar and you're fallin' off the stool."

"You fellows who are gonna have a little fun," he says, "are hurtin' some of the other boys because you're not in the best shape when you come out the next day to play ball." But on the other hand, he was fair. He would say, "Okay, you want to stay out a little later than the rule, you come to me. You come to me and ask permission. Then if I get a call from a sports writer or someone who said they saw you down someplace, I'll say, 'I know all about it, I gave permission.'"

The pattern is about the same for all team managers because they may have to bring up something in a meeting that's outside of baseball. They would have a meeting on a get-away day or the day before. So you bring your bags down to the clubhouse. We're leaving right after the game, right from the park to the railroad station and away we go. We'd have meetings for things like that.

The two managers who influenced me the most were Marty Krug in Los Angeles at the beginning of my career, and Bill McKechnie, my manager in Boston and Cincinnati for nine of my ten full years in the National League.

Marty Krug liked veteran ball players. He didn't really want rookies although he was a good teacher. He wanted a team of guys who knew how to play ball and didn't need too many signs. He had guys like Jigger Statz and Freddie Haney who could hit and run and steal bases, and they ran on their own. They didn't need a signal. They knew the game. They knew when to run.

Despite this, Marty was a pretty good manager even with the young guys, because he was a natural teacher. He really could teach. He would take a young man and work with him. Most managers don't fool around with that. You have to learn the hard way. Trial-and-error and a few chewing-outs, and maybe you learn something.

Krug was particularly good on base running, and was himself a very good base stealer. One year, Marty stole fifty bases out of 52 attempts. He really knew that side of the business! He wasn't running all the time. In those days you stole only when it meant something to be on second base, not just running regardless of the score. You see guys today trying to steal seven runs behind and seven runs ahead. Seven runs either way, you don't want to steal. You can break your leg sliding in, and your run don't mean nothin' when you have a big lead. When you're far behind, your runs are no good, either.

I notice today, watching big-league games on television or at the ball park, that one thing they are bad at today is base running. They make more mistakes base running than anything else they do. I wonder what some of these fellows can be thinking about when they get thrown out at fifteen or twenty feet. You have to have a better than fifty percent chance of making it.

Marty was good at catching the other team's signs, and he would relay them to the batter – fast balls, curves, and the like. At first, he called them for me until I got beaned after he called the wrong pitch. After that, I said to him, "Marty, don't call them for me any more. When I leave you, I'll be helpless. I won't know how to hit on my own." Marty replied, "But that's the first time I ever missed one." "Yeah," I told him, "and it could have been my last!"

There were several reasons I didn't want that kind of help. You want to hit on your own. Suppose they tell you a fast ball is coming and you're ready for it. If it's a little bit high, you're likely to chase it. You'll chase a bad pitch. If you get set for a curve, as I mention elsewhere, you could get killed by a fast ball. It's better to see for yourself.

One time in Boston we were playing an exhibition game, and I was featured as the home-run hitter to get out the crowd. The local catcher wanted to help me, so he said, "Wally, I'll call them for you." He was surprised when I said, "No thanks. Try to fool me. Don't let me know what's coming."

I have to admit that one time at Boston during a double header, I got the signs and I hit three home runs in about five or six at-bats by knowing what was coming, but generally I preferred to figure my own way out.

They used to figure that the curve ball was the toughest ball to hit. However, if it was in the right location, if it was in the corner down around my knees, I could pull the ball to left field.

Thinking about this reminds me of the time I was playing against New York when McGraw was the manager. He kept telling his pitchers to throw me the curve, and I kept hitting it out of the park. I was so surprised that he didn't change that I blurted out to the catcher, "For God's sake, he's supposed to be the smartest manager in baseball. How come he keeps throwing me the curve?"

After a short time in the big leagues, I learned that the fast ball usually wasn't going to be a good pitch. I waited for the curve because I figured it was going to be around the plate, and I was ready to hit it. I looked for that curve for eleven years, and I seldom got crossed up.

A manager whose style I didn't like was Doc Prothro. In Philadelphia, for instance, there was a situation that called for a bunt-sacrifice. There was a man on first and second. So he called me off the bench and wanted me to go up there; I thought I was gonna hit. As I was walking to the plate, he came down the line and said, "Can you bunt?"

And I says, "Listen, Mr. Prothro, I bunted about three times in eleven years. They never called on me to bunt." I shouldn't have said anything and should have gone up there anyhow and fouled off the bunts and then swung away. See, I told him what I thought, so he called up Joe Marty in my place. Marty did just what I should have done. He bunted the first one foul. Then he looked down at the manager and got the hit sign.

Another time, the Phillies were down in last place. They had a young prospect, and the club wasn't going anywhere. The manager put a young left-hander in the game. So right away he had a guy warming up in the bull pen. I'm sitting down there with the rest of the guys (to get away from the dugout), and I said, "Look at that, he's building up that kid's confidence by starting him in a game, and he's already got another guy warming up." And sure enough, the kid walked a couple or three and the manager yanked him out of the game.

The kid was nervous, but the manager didn't give him a chance. I didn't like that. I thought it was lousy. Now this thing sticks in my mind – I'd have pitched the kid, let him pitch the whole damn thing and let the other team get five runs off him, because if you thought enough of him to bring him up and start him in a game, you ought to let him go out there. Let him get baptized.

F. "Okay, Let's Play Ball!"

Bill Klem was the greatest umpire I ever saw. I had confidence in him when I was up there hitting. He had an uncanny judgment on balls and strikes. If it was an inch outside, it was a ball. That's how close he could call them.

When Klem was head umpire, he ran the game. He had the guts. If he ejected a player or manager from the game, he meant out of the dugout and off the field. He watched and made sure that they went *all* the way to the clubhouse. They knew that they would forfeit the game if they didn't obey his instructions. That would cost them the game. It also meant a thousand-dollar fine, so they would give in.

He had two techniques which let the complainers know how far they could go. If they came storming down breathing fire, he would literally draw the line. He'd drag his foot in the dirt and make a line. Then he would say, "Step across that line and it'll cost you a hundred dollars."

Usually they would then continue arguing and shouting four or five feet away from him. He'd let it go on for a minute or two. Then he would pull his watch out of his pocket and give his next warning: "You've got one minute to get back to the dugout or I'm going to forfeit the game."

When I first came up to Boston, Klem was umpiring a game, and a player whispered to me, "Hey, Wally, call him 'Catfish.'" Another player warned me quickly, saying, "Don't do it, Wally. If you call him 'Catfish,' you'll be a marked man with him as long as you're in this League. It really burns him up." The nickname was given to him because of the shape of his mouth – behind his back, of course, but he knew about it and it made him very angry.

Klem also used to say, "I'm the king. Klem is the king." And he'd sing a little ditty back there when he called strike two: "You can't hit the ball with the bat on your shoulder." He was right, of course. If they are close enough to call, they're close enough to hit: an old baseball saying. I used to say it to myself as a reminder.

In hitting, there's a little border line. Sometimes it was only a matter of an inch or two – high or low, inside or outside. They used to pitch me kind of high when I first started playing. I would chase high fast balls. As I became more experienced, I got to lay off that ball because it's a pitcher's pitch. You're likely to fly out or strike out on it.

Umpires get tired of chronic bitchers. We had one on the Boston team who was crabbing all the time. I learned about their feelings regarding certain players from Bill Delaney, a concession manager in Boston, who was friendly to me. He entertained the umpires when they were in town. Bill was a bachelor who had a nice suite of rooms in an apartment house, and he'd invite the umpires over for drinks and cold cuts.

Umpires will usually listen quietly to a legitimate gripe, and then they'd say, "Okay, let's play ball." But the guy who takes a third strike and complains loudly is using a kind of alibi at the ump's expense. Most players just walk away when they get a called third strike. Why holler about it? It doesn't fool anyone.

Sometimes when things go wrong with a club, they take it out on the umpires by beefing. That happened once with the Giants and I joined in. Klem turned to me and said, "And you, too?" What he meant, I believe, was that I seldom complained unless I thought it was a little too raw.

However, I never used foul language with the umpires. I would back out of the box, but I wouldn't look at them when I said, "God damn it, that ball was too high, or it was too low, or it was outside." If you turn your head, look at the umpire and complain, particularly if you're at home, the crowd picks it up and gives the umpire hell the rest of the day. So I got along with the umpires.

"Beans" Reardon, another famous umpire of the Thirties, once went out of his way to help me. I had squawked about a ball being a little too low. I was in a slump at the time, and that's probably why I did it. The next day when the umpires came out, he stopped me and said, "Wally, you hollered about a pitch yesterday. It was a good pitch. Right over. Know what you're doing? You're jerking your head up a little. You're not following the ball and it looks a little low to you."

I responded, "Thanks, Beans; I appreciate that." The next time I got up to the plate, I paid attention and followed the ball longer. I started hitting again. By God, that was it! Beans was right!

Most players would tell you that they wouldn't take the job of umpire for anything in the world. You've got to have a thick skin to be an umpire. You catch hell from both sides in the stands. You can't please everyone. You can't listen to that crowd and let it get to you. We really respected the umpires; most of the bitching was just part of the game.

ELEVEN

SOUVENIRS

A. A Souvenir from George Herman Ruth (1895-1948)

Wally saw Babe Ruth for the first time when he was a high-school student in San Francisco. A decade later, he played against Ruth in spring training in St. Petersburg in his rookie year, and for a number of years thereafter. Wally is featured with the Babe in a brochure which advertises the series between the Yankees and the Braves in St. Petersburg in 1933.

Wally, who wore the same number (three) on his uniform with the Braves as Ruth had worn in his great days with the Yankees, yielded his number gracefully to the great one. He played next to Babe in the outfield and tried to support him with youth and speed. He witnessed close up the fall of the mightiest player of them all.

Wally's story here is mainly about the last days of Babe Ruth – a tragicomedy played out in Boston in the early months of the 1935 season.

When Babe Ruth was in his prime – and his prime lasted a long time – attention on the field was always focused on him. We used to joke about it and say that if you were a player on the Yankees and were going bad, nobody noticed. Everyone was watching The Babe.

He had all the pressure but he didn't know it. It didn't bother him. On the day of a game, he didn't know who was pitching against the Yankees – and he didn't care. His teammates weren't likely to slump as long as the Babe was in there.

Ruth liked to have fun and he liked his drinks. When he was with us that last season in Boston, he carried his bottles with him in a suitcase. He chewed tobacco regularly on the field and he loved hot dogs and ate a lot of them. In his last few years, as can be seen in his pictures, he got pretty heavy.

One year in spring training, he came up with a bad stomach.

153

He'd be up there at batting practice, and he'd stop and yell to the trainer, "Hey, Jimmie, bring me my milk!" The trainer would send out the clubhouse boy with a glass of white stuff (probably Milk of Magnesia). He'd call time, drink the liquid, belch a few times and give the glass back. Then he would continue batting practice.

No one else looked like Babe Ruth. He was a familiar figure to millions. Writers were always calling attention to his "spindly legs." They were exaggerating. His legs weren't spindly. They just didn't seem to fit with the rest of his body. He had a big torso, great big shoulders and a big chest. The way he wore his pants made his legs look thinner, but they were strong and he ran well.

The Babe was smart in his own way – not like a Phi Beta Kappa, but just day-to-day smartness from his experience with people. His intelligence stopped cold when it came to money matters, however. He liked the ponies and he liked women and he spent his money like it was never going to quit coming in.

The smartest thing he did with regard to money was to allow the Christy Walsh Management firm to handle it for him. (That was the outfit that got me a hundred dollars a year to endorse Wheaties – "The Breakfast of Champions.") Walsh invested Babe's money for him in some kind of trust fund and put him on a budget. The money must have been invested well because Babe lived comfortably in retirement. When he died, his wife, Claire, seemed to have enough money to live very well.

I never socialized with Ruth. When a game was over, he went his own way. After all, he was in demand; he was such a powerhouse. He knew big, important people – governors, mayors and businessmen who liked to be seen with him.

Often, before or after a game, he would stop by an orphanage or hospital, visiting kids and autographing things for them. He gave me his unlisted number and told me to call him when I was in New York, but I never did.

Today, almost any player who does something well is referred to as a superstar. We didn't use that term in the Thirties, but The Babe would have deserved the title because he was good in every department of the game. Of course his hitting overshadowed everything else, so that people tend to forget that he was a great pitcher, a good outfielder and a competent first baseman.

He was no Joe DiMaggio out there, but he was good. He had a good, accurate arm and was a good base-runner. When he was thirty-five years old in 1930, he had 266 putouts in right field and ten assists – all this while he scored 150 runs and batted in 153 runs in 145 games.

Babe also had a good eye at the plate. He drew 136 bases on balls that year (he leads all hitters in walks – 2,056 during his career), while still hitting 49 home runs. Pitchers, of course, tried to be careful pitching to him!

To top it off, Babe stole ten bases in 1930 and a total of 123 during his career. Contrast this figure with those for Earl Combs (76), Earl Averill (69), Chick Hafey (70), Vince DiMaggio (79), and Joe DiMaggio (30).

Most fans knew that Ruth began his career as a pitcher with the Red Sox in faraway Boston, but few realize what a great pitcher he was. In the four years when he was primarily a pitcher, he won 78 games and lost forty. Just to make the point, a few statistics. Let's compare his pitching record with the great left-hander and Hall-of-Famer Sandy Koufax:

CAREER AS PITCHER

KOUFAX: Won 165, lost 87; percentage .655.
               Earned run average: 2.76

RUTH: Won 94, lost 46; percentage .671.
               Earned run average: 2.28.

WORLD SERIES

KOUFAX: *(4 years)* Won 4, lost 3;
                           earned run average 0.95.

RUTH: *(2 years)* Won 3, lost 0;
                           earned run average 0.88.

I first saw Babe Ruth when he came to San Francisco after he had established a new record for home runs in 1919. He hit 29! Imagine that – an incredible 29 home runs. The next year, he hit 54. He pitched in only one game and played 142 games in the outfield and at first base. By the way, he won the game in which he pitched, although he lasted only four innings.

So The Babe came barnstorming. It was in 1920, I think. I was still in high school and I went down to the old Seals Park to see him. He wasn't heavy, then. He was lean and tough.

Well, he put on a one-man batting show. He brought his own batting practice pitcher with him – who threw the ball to Ruth right in his alley, one after another. Babe hit them so far almost every time that they went over the fence down Valencia Street. The people who saw him used to say that the balls went all the way down to the Valencia Street Theater, which was about six blocks away. They were exaggerating, but the way he hit them made the ball park look small.

And I never saw anyone, before or since, hit them consistently as far as Babe did. All the big power hitters can hit them, one here and one there, as far as Ruth did, but Ruth could hit them consistently. I'm talking about 500-footers. It surprised me to hear that he never hit one over Yankee Stadium. He never cleared the right field roof. I think Mantle hit the top of it, and Ruth probably did, too, but no one has ever hit clear out. Babe hit some into the center field bleachers – a country mile away from the batter's box at 466 feet just to the fence.

In my first year with the Braves, we played a series with the Yankees at St. Petersburg, as we did each year in spring training for a number of years. By 1933, I was well-established with the Braves, and the flyer announcing the series featured Ruth and me.

The first time I played against the Babe, I was in left field. I played him as far out in left field as I would play a strong right-handed power hitter. He not only hit the ball far; he hit it high – "high sky," we called it. In Florida, a "high sky" is where there isn't a cloud. There's no background.

Ruth would get under one and you'd stand there, and it would look like an aspirin tablet up there. I'd wait for it to come down. Finally, I'd realize that I was catching up high, staggering all over the place. When The Babe came up, I'd think, "Don't hit it out here, Babe, it'll hit the top of my head!"

In 1935 Babe Ruth returned to Boston, this time with the Braves. (He began his major-league career there with the Red Sox in 1914.) He reached the end of the line with the Yankees in the 1934 season. He wanted to manage the Yankees, but management wanted him to begin with a minor-league club. I heard that he was offered the job of managing Newark, the Yankee team across the river, and that he refused.

Judge Fuchs and the Braves were in big financial trouble.

With the Yankees being in an embarrassing situation, the Judge sensed an opportunity to save the Braves. He used the same ploy that he dreamed up when he first purchased the team in 1923. At that time he convinced the great pitcher, Christy Mathewson, to become President of the Braves, with himself as Vice-President.

The Judge's offer to Ruth in a letter quoted by Harold Kaese in his book, *The Boston Braves* (1948), reminded me of the kind of letters The Judge used to write to me when we were arguing about salary:

"...In consideration of this offer, the Boston Club naturally will expect you to do everything in your power for the welfare and interest of the Club and will expect that you will endeavor to play in the games whenever possible, as well as carry out the duties specified above.

"...If it was determined, after your affiliation with the ball club in 1935, that it was for the mutual interest of the club for you to take up the active management on the field, there would be absolutely no handicap in having you so appointed..."

In other words, The Judge got Ruth to sign by leading him to believe that he would eventually get the manager's job. He got the titles of assistant manager and vice-president. His salary was to be $25,000, just twice what I was then making. Bill McKechnie, of course, was still manager, and he was pretty popular around Boston. Fuchs was in a ticklish situation. He had to figure out how to get rid of McKechnie without having all the fans and newspapers on him.

What The Judge had in mind was to use Babe as the drawing card – pack 'em in. He wanted him to play every Saturday and Sunday, and show up during the week for batting practice. We didn't ordinarily draw on weekdays – three thousand would be a good crowd. People saved their money for the Saturday game or for the double-header on Sunday. If we were going fairly good during the week, we might hit thirty or forty thousand on the weekend.

Fuchs evidently tried to get Ruth to invest some of his money in the Braves. I overheard part of a conversation between them, riding back to Boston with them from Worcester one afternoon.

Before we opened the season each year, we would play a game at Holy Cross in Worcester, about forty or fifty miles down the road from Boston. This afternoon, Ruth played only three or four innings. Bill Urbanski and I also finished early. When we got outside, we saw Ruth and The Judge sitting in the front seat of The

Babe's sixteen-cylinder Cadillac. It was a big, luxurious car – like a limousine. (Cadillac had made a V-8 as early as 1914, and by 1930 had experimented with both twelve- and sixteen-cylinder cars.)

Calling over to Ruth, I asked, "Babe, how about a ride back with you?" "Sure," he replied, "hop in." Soon we were driving up the Worcester Turnpike, a kind of early freeway. Ruth was driving fast. I peered over the seatback to get a look at the speedometer – we were going ninety miles an hour! In that big, heavy Cadillac, you didn't realize that you were moving so fast.

The Judge and Babe were having a big discussion and talking pretty loud. It seemed that The Judge was making a proposal to The Babe about investing in some way, but I couldn't hear all the details, but I did hear Ruth disagreeing with Fuchs – finally he cut The Judge short by saying bluntly, "Judge, I take. I don't give." That ended their conversation for the moment, and, to my relief, Babe turned his concentration back to driving.

In his 41st year, Babe could still hit them a mile. As for his being over the hill with the Yankees in 1934, it's all relative. For Ruth, yes, but for most of the outfielders in the majors right now, it wouldn't seem bad. He played in 125 games, compiling a batting average of .288 and a slugging percentage of .537, a figure most outfielders never reach in their entire career. He scored 78 runs and batted in 84. He was in the outfield for 111 games and had 197 putouts and three assists for 208 total chances. He made eight errors--and even stole a base! Forty-three of 105 hits were for extra bases – twenty-two of them were home runs.

On our way to Boston from spring training in 1935, we stopped and played Newark in an exhibition game. Babe hit one that day clear out of center field about fifty feet over the center field fence.

He started the game against the Giants on opening day. Carl Hubbell was pitching. They all played Ruth deep. He hit a tremendously hard line drive past Bill Terry, about three feet off the ground...Bill just gave it the "how do you do?" His glove went down and up quickly; if he had challenged it, the ball would have knocked off his hand.

Later in the game, old Babe said, "Watch me tap one into left field." He was just going to single to left – he could always hit to the opposite field. So he tapped one into the left field bleachers 375 feet away! His "tap" was a good drive for

158

a powerful right-hand hitter.

On May 21, in Chicago, he hit his third home run, and on May 25, in Pittsburgh, for the second time in his career, he hit three home runs in a single game (he also hit a single). All told, he knocked in six runs, but we still lost the game 11 to 7; that was the kind of year it was going to be.

Although Ruth could still hit, his legs were giving out. His eyesight was good and his timing was good, but he couldn't play the outfield very well. He had two bum knees and two bum ankles. I played center and he played left. Every time a ball was hit in his direction, I had to move over there to back him up. I was afraid it was either going to go through him or that he was going to misplay it.

If anything went wrong defensively, say he misjudged one that went over his head and hit the fence, and I picked it up and fired it in, he'd just walk right off the field. His fielding glove was a little white one. The players used to kid him about it, called it a "motorman's glove" because it resembled the one worn by motormen on the trolley cars. Well, Babe would roll up that little glove, stuff it into his back pocket and walk off the field. He did it at least three times that I remember: in Philadelphia, Cincinnati, and once in Boston.

At first, the Braves management went out of their way to make Ruth happy. Two incidents may illustrate the way they catered to him.

In the first instance, it was a very humorous situation as far as the other players were concerned – but not to The Babe. One day, the great Ruth had to use the toilet in the Boston club house, but there was only one toilet – and it was occupied by Randy Moore, who was sitting in there, leisurely reading the paper. The Babe paced up and down. Randy continued to read his paper. Finally, Ruth angrily picked up the phone and called the office. They evidently listened politely as Babe yelled into the phone: "It's ridiculous to have only one Goddam crapper in the clubhouse. I want another one put in here right away!"

That was Vice-President Ruth talking. We all wondered what would happen – and it didn't take long to find out. The next day, the plumbers came and installed crapper number two.

In the second instance, some of the players were telling Ruth about the background in center field. They told him that it was pretty good, except on warm days when all the fans were

159

wearing white shirts, then it was hard for the batters to see the ball. The Vice-President said to them, "We'll do something about this," so he called the office and told them, "The boys can't see the ball very well with all those white shirts in center field. I want a green background for center field." Within a few days, a crew came and painted a green background.

It was getting down to June, and Ruth still hadn't been "promoted" to the manager's job. He made it clear that he didn't intend to play every day. Fuchs kept pressing him to play even in meaningless exhibition games, but Babe understood what The Judge was doing – and began to resent it.

He complained that he didn't come to Boston to play regularly. He never did try to interfere in any way with McKechnie's running of the club. He never asserted himself as "assistant manager." And he played only one full game in the National League.

There is another thing about the year that Ruth came to Boston. We wound up with the worst record of any major-league team in the 20th Century, and Ruth had a lot to do with it – not directly, and it wasn't his fault.

He came to Boston thinking that he was going to manage the club, which was what The Judge didn't know how to handle. You don't promise Ruth a job and not give it to him, and it is particularly embarrassing when you already have a highly respected manager in that job.

In this situation, moreover, there were two sets of rules: one for Babe Ruth and one for the rest of the team. It affected morale. You could see that Bill McKechnie was down in the dumps because of internal problems, but he kept his calm. He got so that he just let us play ball. It was pretty hard to discipline a player for drinking, for example, when The Babe could do what he wanted.

The event which led to Ruth's departure from the Braves was the arrival of the great French liner, *Normandie,* in New York. In honor of the new ship's maiden voyage, Ruth was invited to be a member of the committee to greet the *Normandie* as a kind of ambassador of baseball.

Judge Fuchs announced that he would not give Ruth permission to go to New York, which seemed absurd – Fuchs must have wanted him to quit. You don't tell the "Sultan of Swat" that he cannot perform his ceremonial functions. As you might imagine, Babe went anyway. And when he got back, he announced his retirement. Perhaps The Judge was relieved, because things were not turning out the way he hoped. It was obvious that Babe Ruth was not going to save him or the Braves.

Ruth took his last time at bat in the opening game on Memorial Day in Philadelphia. Jim Bivin was the pitcher who had the honor of retiring him. It was no doubt the high point of Bivin's career, since it was his first and only year in the majors.

Before the game with the Giants at Braves Field on June 2, Ruth told us in the clubhouse that he was quitting. I said to myself, "This is a big occasion involving the greatest ball player who ever lived." I grabbed a new baseball and asked him to autograph it for me. I still have it, but it's getting a bit faded because of the ink used in those days. I looked over at his locker, where he had about a dozen bats and asked, "Babe, can I take one of your bats?"

He answered, "Help yourself." So I took one that he had used – it had the scuff mark where he had hit the ball. It's hanging now in my den, along with other memorabilia, including several pictures of me taken with The Babe in spring training.

NOTE: Quotations from the commentary on the Boston Braves in the *Reach Official Base Ball Guide, 1936*. "A summary of the 1935 season."

"President Emil Fuchs severed his connection with the club in August and the franchise was virtually operated by the National League until mid-winter...

"There is little need to dwell any further on this matter, except to say that in the face of troubles that would have completely distracted the average manager, Bill McKechnie gallantly stood by his guns to the finish."

SCHEDULE AND ROSTER
YANKEES and BRAVES

BABE RUTH

HOME RUN
KING
OF YANKEES

• •

WALTER BERGER

LONG
DISTANCE
HITTER
OF BRAVES

• •

1933

Spring Training Camps
ST. PETERSBURG, FLA.

ALL GAMES PLAYED
WATERFRONT PARK

 18

MAJOR LEAGUE GAMES

WATERFRONT PARK

1933—Schedule—1933

BRAVES VS.

Tuesday	March 14	Yankees
Wednesday	March 15	Yankees
Thursday	March 16	Yankees
Friday	March 17	Philadelphia
Saturday	March 18	Cardinals
Sunday	March 19	Yankees
Monday	March 20	Cardinals
Tuesday	March 21	Yankees
Thursday	March 23	Yankees
Friday	March 24	Yankees
Saturday	March 25	Yankees
Sunday	March 26	Yankees
Thursday	March 30	Newark
Saturday	April 1	Cincinnati

YANKEES VS.

Wednesday	March 22	Cardinals
Monday	March 27	Cincinnati
Tuesday	March 28	Newark
Wednesday	March 29	House of David

ALL GAMES BEGIN AT 3 O'CLOCK

18

B. Manager Deacon Bill McKechnie, Leader and Survivor

William Boyd McKechnie was a survivor. He survived as a mediocre player for eleven years in the period 1907-1920. As an infielder, he played a majority of his games at third base, and as manager was seldom satisfied – Wally says – with the performance of anyone at that position. He played with Pittsburgh and Cincinnati, and, in between, with the Indiana Federals and the Newark Federals. He managed Newark for ninety-nine games in 1915.

The "Deacon" also survived as a manager in the National League for twenty-five years (1922-1946). He rode up and down that roller coaster in Pittsburgh, St. Louis, Boston and Cincinnati. He reached the top the first time in Pittsburgh in 1925, when the Pirates won the National League pennant and then defeated Washington (4-3) in the World Series. The next year he dropped to third place, only four-and-a-half games out of first, and he was fired.

In 1927, he became a coach in St. Louis. Catcher Bob O'Farrell, the manager, finished in second place, only one-and-one-half games behind Pittsburgh. He was fired, and McKechnie replaced him. In 1928, McKechnie led them to a league championship, but lost four straight to the Yankees in the World Series. Thereupon he was sent forthwith to their farm in Rochester, and Billy Southworth was given the job. Billy stumbled and McKechnie was brought back at mid-season. In 1929, St. Louis finished in fourth place, twenty games out of first place.

McKechnie departed from St. Louis when owner Judge Fuchs, who had taken over as his own manager with disastrous results, offered him a five-year contract to manage Boston. He arrived in Boston in 1930, the same year that the Braves bought Wally Berger from Los Angeles. Wally hit thirty-eight home runs and batted in 119. The Braves moved from last to sixth place. In 1931, they dropped to seventh place. In 1933, Wally put them in fourth place with a grand-slam home run in the last game of the season. In 1934, they stayed in fourth place.

In 1935, ten years after having reached the pinnacle in Pittsburgh, McKechnie's roller coaster hit bottom in Boston. The Braves finished in last place with the worst record of any team in the 20th Century. However, this time McKechnie was not fired. For once in baseball history it was the owner who left – not the manager

164

– under circumstances so dire that no one in Boston blamed the manager. In fact, the *Spalding Guide*, in its annual report, paid McKechnie an unusual tribute, recognizing his ability to survive the season.

Boston bounced back with McKechnie to sixth place in 1936, and to fifth place in 1937. His efforts were so admired that two offers came to him that year – one from fifth-place Cleveland in the American League and the other from last-place Cincinnati in the National League. McKechnie chose Cincinnati.

McKechnie later explained his choice to Wally. "I picked Cincinnati," he said, "because they were down at the bottom, and at the bottom any improvement is good. If you move up a couple of notches, that's very good. On the other hand, if you go to a club that's up there, you've got to stay there. You can't afford to have a bad year. You take a tail-end club and improve their position and you've done a good job managing."

The Deacon was right. He took Cincinnati to fourth place in 1938 as Wally joined him there that year. He won the National League Pennant in 1939, but lost to New York in the World Series. In 1940, he won the league championship and the World Series – again, he had reached the top. He stayed in Cincinnati until 1946; the next year he left for Cleveland to coach. Then he retired to the warmth of Florida – where he died at the age of 79 in 1965, having survived most of his contemporaries in baseball.

McKechnie was a silent type of manager, very low-key. He had played third base for Pittsburgh way back in 1915 or something like that. He was a man you respected, and you played hard because of your respect for the man. He was not a John McGraw type, a driver, but you knew he meant what he said. You respected him for that because you knew what would happen if you violated anything. He could really hurt you like he said he would – in your pocketbook. No, he was a gentleman, a very nice man. I loved to play for him. In fact, when I managed for a couple of years, I patterned a little bit off of McKechnie, using his style.

He was great in handling pitchers. And he was more a defensive man – good pitching, good defense – play for one run early, "Just keep getting one run at a time and we'll get four runs – and we'll win." This was his style until he got to Cincinnati. There he had all these pretty good hitters and a smaller, short left-field fence, so he let it go the other way and played for a lot of runs. With power on the club, a lot of hitters, he played it the other way. He played, I guess, for the ball park and the team he had. (Remember that Boston had a big ball park where it was hard to hit home runs.)

Bill McKechnie never got too close to the players. He stood aside as if to say, "I'm the boss; I'm the manager." He went out of his way not to show favoritism. Even if he liked you, he still kept aloof.

He didn't socialize much. I did go to the theater with him one time in New York. His brother was in the theatrical business. He was a producer or something, and gave Bill tickets for a show on Broadway with Frederic March. It was a legitimate play and he asked me to go to that.

I did go to his house for dinner on #1 Scenery Road in Wilkinsburg up on the hill – he had a nice house up there. He invited me for dinner and showed me all his guns. He liked to hunt, and he was really proud of his collection of rifles and shotguns. He had a showcase there. After dinner, he poured me a glass of wine and said, "I guess you'd like to get back to the hotel to be with your player friends."

I said, "Yeah, I think I'll shove off, Bill." I wasn't at ease; I really wanted to be with the fellows. I never fooled around with the front office – never did. I never played that part of it. I stayed with the players; I was for the players. I didn't want to be known as a guy who's sucking someone's tit up there in the office.

In negotiations, I understood McKechnie's position. He was sort of caught in the middle. I was dealing with Judge Fuchs by mail, phone and wire. When the Judge came down from Boston to Richmond, Virginia, to the Murphy Hotel there, he was interviewing about half-a-dozen hold-outs and he was taking them around one at a time. It was getting near the opening of the season and he had to sign up these fellows. I was the last one called into the room— and there was McKechnie. That was the only time he got into it. He sided with the Judge. He told me he thought they were giving me a square deal – that I should sign – and I replied, "No, Bill, I don't think it's a square deal."

The Judge wanted McKechnie to influence me. I did like McKechnie very much and it did bother me. I'm German, and I'm stubborn, and when I made up my mind not to do something, that was it. No one could have persuaded me to change my mind.

The only time in our long association that I was disappointed in McKechnie, and even a little sad, was during spring

166

training in 1940. This was the year that Warren Giles gave me my unconditional release. Bill, for some reason, behaved very strangely. I was treated in a way that I thought was deliberate humiliation, and Bill did not take time to say goodbye.

Here are several situations which show how McKechnie handled discipline problems. The first one involved "Wee Willie" Sherdel. McKechnie told us that story. In the cases of Ed Brandt and Whitey Moore, I was an eyewitness.

In Boston, most of the team liked to sleep in as long as they could. There was no morning call. Games were usually scheduled for 3:00 in the afternoon. They figured you ought to be up by 9:00 – maybe 10:00 – but I was up and in the dining room at 7:00, which stems back to my working days when I had to get up early in the morning.

The hotel dining rooms opened at 6:00. One time I walked into the dining room at St. Louis at 7:00 a.m., and who is there but Bill McKechnie having breakfast. He says, "What are you doing, just getting in?" I said, "Come on, Bill, you know I'm an early riser." I knew he was, too, because he was an insomniac, and he'd let the players know that.

He said, "There's a lot of times I go to bed, but I get up at midnight and take a walk and sit in the lobby for a little while. That's how I catch some of these players coming in after hours." He always left the team with the thought that he might be in the lobby when they did show up.

McKechnie told a story which explains how he dealt with the night-owls. He was sitting up waiting for Grover Cleveland Alexander, who was a drinker. He waited until one or two in the morning. Then he said to himself, "To hell with Alexander; I might as well go up and try to sleep." He got into the elevator, and as the operator tried to close the door, someone yelled, "Hold the door!" In walked Wee Willie Sherdel, his prize left-handed pitcher.

McKechnie didn't say a thing. Sherdel didn't say nothing. He got off at his floor. The next day in the club house McKechnie made the lineup and told Sherdel he was pitching. It wasn't Sherdel's turn, but he knew what McKechnie meant. He knew he'd better win that ball game.

It was a hot day and Willie had come home at 2:00 a.m., so McKechnie pitched him...that was one of his standard deals. If he knew you were out late, he'd pitch you right out of turn.

Bill did it to another guy in Brooklyn one time on a really hot day. Eddie Brandt and I were out on the town in New York. Brandt was laughing and having a good time. We went to a nightclub or two, and McKechnie got wind of our adventures. He said, "Brandt, you're pitching."

Brandt won the game, but he struggled. I could see from the outfield that his ass was wet and his shirt was soaked and wet. Those beers were coming out. I suffered through it, too. I think I got a couple of hits. I had to get some hits because Bill knew I was with Brandt – it was my punishment, too. I'll tell you – we went to bed early that night!

In 1939 when I was with Cincinnati, I saw Bill really get angry with Whitey Moore, but it was a controlled anger. Whitey was a starting pitcher, but McKechnie said to Whitey, "I need a relief pitcher." Whitey was a good fast ball pitcher with fairly good control. McKechnie reassured him, saying, "You'll get the same money; don't worry about it. I'll take care of you, but I need that good stopper out there."

Whitey went out in the game and they battered him. He came back, threw his glove into the dugout and kicked the water coolers. McKechnie came over and said, "Take it easy now, Whitey." He already knew what the fellow was gonna do – Whitey stormed outta there, got into his clothes, left the ball park, got into his car and went out and got drunk. His car stalled on the railroad track. He got pinched and they threw him in jail.

This was gettin' down to the end of the season when we're fighting for the pennant. We heard that Whitey had been arrested. Everyone was waiting for the meeting – we knew this was gonna be a classic, but how was McKechnie going to handle the situation?

Everyone was quiet when he started talking. He started talking really nice and slow like nothing's going to happen. He finally said, "Whitey, you let down all your fellow players – you let them down. We are fighting for the pennant, and what do you do? You get yourself arrested."

Then it started building up. He started getting louder and louder, and Whitey said, "You oughta send me..." McKechnie interrupted him and said, "Goddamn you, I'm gonna send you out as for as I can send you and you'll never get back." And by that time he was really in high pitch.

I can't remember the whole speech; I wish I had it recorded. But it was good, and they got Whitey off, got him out on bail. They

168

arranged with the court to try him after the World Series – and he was gonna go in front of a judge who hated drunken drivers.

After all that, we were going up to Yankee Stadium, and as Whitey was coming over to our cab, the local kids spotted him and pointed at him. You know the New York kids; they shout, "There's Whitey Moore!" Whitey says, "They didn't know I was around until I got arrested, but now they know me."

After the Series they did have the trial, and Whitey had to spend a couple of days in jail.

McKechnie reprimanded me only two times that I can remember, and both times I disagreed with him. I guess the view from the bench is a little different.

Both involved base running. One time in St. Louis, I was on first and it was a ground ball, one that looked like a double play, and Frankie Frisch was playing second. He was a smart second baseman, one of the best. I started to slide to my right. Frisch saw me coming and he cut across as if he was going to throw from the other side of the bag, I changed my slide. It was very dangerous to change your slide the last second, and I hit that bag hard, because I slid late doing it. McKechnie chided me by saying, "If you'd broke up that double play, we would have..."

I stopped him and said, "God damnit, I liked to have broken both legs trying to break up that double play. Besides, that guy's getting $40,000 a year. He's no dummy out there."

McKechnie gave me hell anyway, and it burned me up. I very seldom ever got mad at myself, but if I think I'm being ridiculed unfairly, I'll get mad about that. I don't like that. If I think I'm right, I'm gonna get into an argument. I thought he was wrong for saying that because I knew damn well I was trying to break up the double play – and I always tried to break up double plays – but this time I could have hurt myself by making a change.

You see, the second baseman could field the ball. He could go to the bag, touch it, back off and throw. Either that or he touches the bag and goes to the inside – to the infield side – and throws from there. I started to slide to the right (outside) and he just went across the bag, and I tried to change and follow him, but it didn't do any good.

The baseman's not gonna stay on the bag unless you hit 'em. They're off the bag, on and off one way or the other. I had done my best to break up the double play the way I thought right, and it burned me up when McKechnie claimed I hadn't tried.

Another time he did say something to me. I was on second base; whenever you get on base, you look around to see who the outfielders are and where everyone is playing. You don't have time to think if you're going to go at the crack of the bat. Well, I looked behind me and saw that the short stop was shading me over toward second base. That's the last thing I saw. A line drive went by, and I thought it went right to the short stop, but he had moved back to his regular position and the ball went by him, but I hesitated and didn't score. McKechnie commented, "That's the first mistake you've made on the bases in ten years."

I considered myself a good base runner and I said, "Well, Bill, that short stop crossed me up there. I thought he was right where that line drive went, and I didn't want to be doubled up." That's a pretty good working relationship between player and manager – two disagreements on the field in nine years.

C. A Brief Encounter with the Great Satchel Paige

The Philadelphia Colored Giants (Royal Giants) came to Los Angeles for the winter. It was like barnstorming; they would pick up extra money. They had a terrific team – a number of them could have played in the big leagues, but no one was scouting or hiring black ball players.

Organized baseball "drew the color line," as the expression went in those days. There were no black players in the major leagues until after World War II, when the Brooklyn Dodgers signed Jackie Robinson.

One of the Royal Giants' great players was Mule Suttles, who was called "The Black Babe Ruth." He was a giant of a man, standing about six-foot-four and weighing probably 220 or 230 pounds. In one winter season of fifteen or sixteen games, he hit thirteen home runs – and he hit them like Ruth: high and far.

At short they had a very good player named Wells. He had played with the St. Louis black club. Dixon, the right fielder, had an arm that would put most outfielders of today to shame. He threw line drives to the plate. Their catcher, Mackey, had a big grin like Gabby Hartnett, and he reminded me of Hartnett. He was a fair hitter, a good receiver, and he had a good arm.

Foster, a good pitcher and a good man, I remember especially, because he came to see me at the club house in Chicago when we were playing the Cubs. There were a number of others who were good, but whose names I can't remember. That was over fifty years ago.

In 1934, I played in another game against the Royal Giants with the Dizzy Dean All-Stars. The great Satchel Paige pitched for the Giants – Dizzy for the All-Stars. The game was played at Wrigley Field before a crowd of 18,000.

Paige could fire the ball. He and Dean were about the same size, and they both pitched the same way with about the same speed—about 95 miles per hour. I saved the clipping on that game because I got the only hits off Satchel – a double and a triple. I'd hit a famous pitcher – teed off on the ball.

The reason I got a double and a triple off him was that I thought he might have a curve ball, so I looked for the curve. I wasn't going to try to kill the ball, so I cut down on my swing and waited to see how he was pitching me.

First he pitched me high, then he raised it, then he brought it down. No curves. He finally got one down a little too low and I hit it off the center field fence. When I hit the double, he followed me around for a second, looked at me and said, "How'd you hit that one?" I got a kick out of that.

Satchel went back to the mound and struck out the next three batters in order – Camilli, Demaree and Lillard. In the fourth inning I got a triple, and he did the same thing. He followed me with his eyes to third. He struck out seven in four innings, and left the game to save his arm for a game against the White Kings on Sunday, or so the reporters said.

Dizzy Dean struck out seven in seven innings and left the game because of cold weather with the score three-to-two in favor of the All-Stars. The All-Stars won in the ninth, 5-4, getting a run off Chet Brewer. He was the pitcher for the Royal Giants the day I hit three home runs and got into trouble with Judge Landis.

On the previous Sunday, Dean pitched for both sides and was both the winning and losing pitcher in an exhibition game between the Major All-Stars and the Coast All-Stars. He pitched the first three innings for the Coast team and the last six for the Majors. The Majors won by a score of 20-12.

Sports writer Bob Ray wrote that Dizzy's cut of the gate was $3,000, which was a lot of money in the thirties.

D. A Message from the Czar

Before he went to the major leagues, Wally had played on Sundays in the winter league in Los Angeles. After his first season with Boston, he returned to Los Angeles and resumed his playing with the Kelley Kars team, managed by Fred Haney.

In his zeal to improve his skills as a center fielder, he continued to play after October 31, in violation of League rules. In a game with the Royal Giants, a barnstorming team of some of the greatest black baseball stars, he hit three home runs, a feat which came to the attention of Judge Landis, the Commissioner of Baseball, who warned him that he was violating his contract, and reminded him of the fine which could be assessed. Wally went to Fred Haney and asked him how he should respond to the Judge.

(A Note on Judge Landis: If Hollywood Central Casting had been looking for a character actor to play the role of a stern and righteous judge, they could not have found anyone who could have better played the role better than Judge Kenesaw Mountain Landis. He looked like a judge, he dressed like a judge, and he played the part on the public stage to fit the expectations of his audience.

Even the Judge's name was colorful. His father lost a leg on Kenesaw Mountain in Georgia during the Civil War, and afterwards gave that name to his son who was born in 1866.

In 1905, President Teddy Roosevelt named him a Federal District Judge. He became nationally known in 1907 when he fined Standard Oil of Indiana $29,240,000 for accepting illegal rebates on shipments of oil from the Chicago and Alton Railroad. It was in the "trust busting" spirit of the Roosevelt Era. Incidentally, this decision was later reversed.

During World War I, the Judge presided at the trials of Industrial Workers of the World (I.W.W.) leaders and Socialists who opposed the war. They were convicted of obstructing the war effort. Shortly thereafter, a bomb exploded at the entrance of the Federal Building where Landis was in his chambers on the sixth floor. His reputation as a fearless and patriotic judge was greatly enhanced as a result of this wartime activity.

When the leaders of major-league baseball, in the wake of the "Black Sox" scandal of 1919 (when players on the Chicago White Sox were accused of throwing the World Series), created the new office of Commissioner of Baseball, they offered the job to

Judge Landis. It was an action planned to improve the image of professional baseball – and it did. But, in the process, baseball got its first and only "Czar." The Judge survived through many a controversy until his death in 1944.

For several years, I played in the winter league in Los Angeles. In 1928, Howard Lindamore was running the Shell Oil team down at Signal Hill, and he asked me to play for them. It was a pretty good job with Shell. They would sign you up as a laborer, but all you did was work out and practice. They would play a couple of games a week. They had a nice ball park, although it had a "skin diamond" (that is to say, a diamond without any grass).

Howard offered me $200 a month to play. When he asked me I sat there thinking it over because I was recovering from intestinal flu, which had put me out of action with the Angels for the last part of the season. I was still weak. Howard thought I was holding out for more money, so he said, "Wally, I'll make it $250."

"No, Howard," I said, "I would have played for $200. It's not the money. My stomach is in bad shape. I've lost twenty pounds. I think I'll just go back home and rest." So I didn't play at all that winter. The next year, 1929, I played a game every Sunday in the winter league.

Near the end of my first year at Boston, after having played left field all season, Manager McKechnie told me that I was going to play center field the next year, an announcement that pleased me greatly. I was the fastest player on the Boston team and I could cover a lot of ground, but I needed to learn to field balls hit at different angles in center field.

When I returned to Los Angeles after the season that fall, I decided to play center field for Kelley Kars in the winter league, just for practice. The manager was Fred Haney, my former teammate and friendly adviser with the Angels.

In those days – in contrast to the present time where you read about major league stars playing everywhere during the winter – we weren't allowed to play exhibition games or anything after October 31.

Well, I played beyond the deadline and I got caught. I had a great day against the Royal Giants, a black all-star team from Philadelphia, and the story went out over the wire services. Judge Landis saw it and sent me a telegram warning me that I was

173

violating the rules and could be fined up to five hundred dollars.

Immediately, I went down to Fred Haney's office to ask his advice. (During the week he worked for an electrical company down at Second and Spring.) "Fred," I said, "I'm in trouble; I'll need your help on this one." I showed him the wire from the Judge.

"We'll send him an answer explaining the circumstances." He told his secretary to take a wire, and he began dictating: "Dear Judge..."

I interrupted him. "Fred, I don't even know the man. How can I say, 'Dear Judge?'"

"Aw, he'll like it," answered Fred, "judges like to be called 'Judge' whether they're still on the bench or not. Once a judge, always a judge."

We composed a telegram and explained that I wasn't playing for money there in the winter league. I was just playing for experience so that I would be a better player for Boston. I followed the wire with a letter explaining the situation in more detail. I never heard anything more from Judge Landis – he let it go. But I quit playing in winter leagues!

I knew that the Judge meant what he said. He really was the Czar of baseball. I remembered that just nine years before, in 1921, when Babe Ruth had become the greatest star in baseball, he ignored the Judge's warning about post-season games after October 31, and went on a barnstorming tour.

The Judge fined the Babe and two other players their full shares earned in the World Series. He also suspended them without pay for the first forty days of the next season.

NEWS REPORT

"Walter Berger, the walloping sensation of the National League, put on a real hitting show at Wrigley Field yesterday afternoon for the Kelley Kars. Although his mates bowed to the Royal Giants, 9 to 8. It was Berger's slugging that featured the tilt. Berger clouted three homers and a single and walked once. His smashes accounted for seven of his team's runs..."

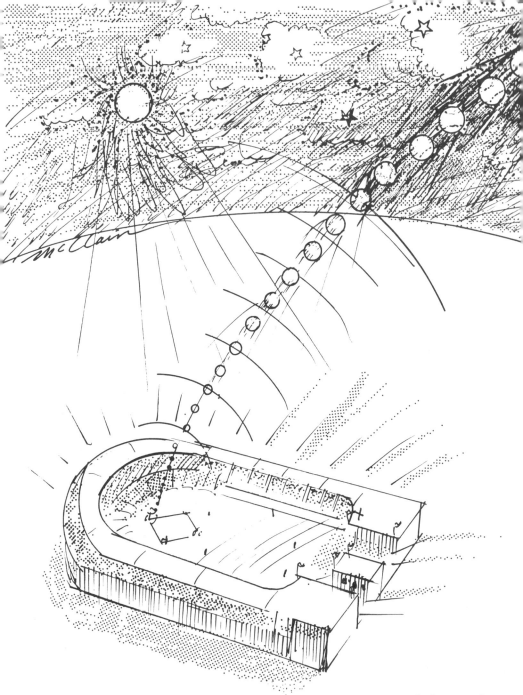

"Berger's bruising belt in the eighth with two on sailed over the roof of the left-field stands where surplus Cub hurlers sun themselves. It was probably the longest homer ever hit at the Polo Grounds, and for all the 20,771 onlookers know, the ball is sailing yet . . ."

TWELVE

A SELF-EVALUATION

A. Berger on Berger

In a recent interview, Zip Dumovich, who played with Wally at Pocatello in 1927 and against him in the Pacific Coast League with Oakland remembered a home run by Wally in the Utah-Idaho League: "I can say one thing. At Pocatello he hit the longest ball I've ever seen hit. When Wally rounded home the outfielder was just getting to the ball."

From high school days on, I was always a long ball hitter. I was pretty good size and I liked to see how far I could hit the ball.

In the Coast League, the manager wanted me to bunt, or fake a bunt, or bunt a foul once every game. He said, "The third baseman's playing you too deep. We want you to fake a bunt or really bunt to beat it out. Otherwise bunt to foul and have that third baseman come in three or four steps." That way I could drive it by him. I bunted often in the Coast League. I was fast and I'd beat out bunts.

When I got to Boston my first year, I thought maybe I could help the club by bunting. I knew that I would get more hits that way. One day I suggested that to George Sisler. I said, "What do you think, George, about me bunting more often?" George looked at me for a minute and answered in what seemed to be a sarcastic tone. He growled, "For Christ's sake, they pay you to hit the ball against the fence or over it. You're not going to bunt. Get up there and hit the ball out of the park!"

That was the advice I got from one of the best hitters in baseball. I'm not sure why he said it. Maybe he thought power was more important to the club, or he was giving me practical advice. At that time I was the only power hitter Boston had.

Sisler was playing his last year, and it was becoming obvious that he had slowed down. Even so, he hit .309 in 116 games, made 133 hits, scored 54 runs, batted in 67 and stole seven bases. At first base he fielded .987, compared with Bill Terry and Jim Bottomley at .990. Not bad for his last year.

Sisler was right; they paid me off for the home run. I knew that Boston bought me from the Angels because I was a long ball hitter, and the papers played up the home run.

Not long after Sisler told me to go for the fence, I was rooming with Johnnie Neun, our first baseman. On one particular day he had four for four, and the newspaper report didn't even include his name. He complained to me, "Hell, I got four for four, and they don't even mention me – just your home runs."

"Well, John, they like to see that long ball. They're paying me for that."

While I hit tape measure home runs in all the parks, the three longest that I remember hitting – and the most satisfying – were hit at Braves Field and at Forbes Field in 1930, and at the Polo Grounds in 1937.

The first one at Braves Field was hit against the Giants. Joe Genewich was pitching. He had knocked me down several times earlier in the game. Coming to bat in the eighth inning with two men on, I guessed a fast ball. I hit it over the bleachers in left center and onto the railroad tracks outside the park. Dead center field at the fence was 425 feet, which gives some idea of how far it traveled.

As I ran around the bases, I taunted Genewich, shouting, "You really had me scared, Joe." It was very satisfying because that hit won the game.

In Pittsburgh that same year, I hit one into left field to the left of the high scoreboard. It cleared the fence by at least fifty feet, and that's pretty deep out there. Chili Doyle, a well-known sportscaster, said that it landed in the fountain. When I went back and looked at the fountain, I said, "My God, did I hit one in there?" Chili replied, "Yes, you did, and it traveled 580 feet." I know that Frank Howard of the Dodgers was supposed to have hit one 580 feet also. Of course, Babe Ruth probably hit a number of them about 600 feet, but I would put him on top in power over anyone.

In 1937, after I was traded to the Giants, I hit one of the longest home runs in my life. In the eighth inning, Charlie Grimm, the Cubs' manager, lifted Bill Lee, a right-hander who had struck out the side in the seventh, and replaced him with Clyde

Shoun, a left-hander.

I couldn't figure his strategy there. Shoun threw pretty fast, so I was expecting a fast ball. I got one right in my slot, and I hit it over the bull pen in deep left center and over the top of the damn Polo Grounds. Here is a description by John Ebinger:

Berger's bruising belt in the eighth with two on sailed over the roof of the left-field stands where surplus Cub hurlers sun themselves. It was probably the longest homer ever hit at the Polo Grounds, and for all the 20,771 onlookers know, the ball is sailing yet...

Bill Terry did something he didn't usually do. He wasn't that kind of guy, but he walked over and waited for me at home plate. When I came around to score, he said, "I've been here since 1923 and that's the longest ball I've ever seen hit here." As I looked up there and thought about it, that really was a mile.

When I'd hit the ball out of the park, I never stopped to admire my handiwork. I'd just hit and start running. Ernie Lombardi (with Cincinnati) used to do that. He'd get a hold of one and he'd look up there for a second or two and say, "Isn't that a beauty?"

Reggie Jackson did it all the time when he connected with one – it thrilled him. Well, it *is* a thrill, because it's perfect timing with all your strength. Everything comes into play, into action. You put the maximum into a swing. It's very satisfying. Babe Ruth sometimes used to stop there and watch them sail out of the park. He used to pause, as if to say, "Wasn't that a dandy?" Well, everybody else stood and watched them, too.

Throughout my career I used a heavy bat – thirty-eight ounces. I never changed the weight. I liked a bat that was thirty-five-and-a-half inches long. I stood on top of the plate, so that I could get that outside pitch, because that was where they were to pitch me. I could pull that outside pitch over the fence.

In my first year, they showed me that I'd have to learn to hit curve balls and off-speed pitches. I could see their pattern and I knew I had to hit them if I was going to stay up there.

They were concentrating on curving me and throwing me the side-arm pitch, which is thrown by a right-handed pitcher to a right-handed batter. They're trying to move you away from the plate by coming by way of third base. If you give a little bit, he throws that ball on the corner and away from your power.

Well, I stayed right up there – I didn't flinch. I didn't give in to the side-arm pitch. Even if they tried to intimidate me by throwing at me, I'd get right up. I used to crowd the plate, and they didn't like it. They wanted the outside corner to work on, and I wouldn't give it to them. So the pattern is a fast ball high and inside to back you off, the side-arm fast ball and then curve balls down and away. They "pulled the string," as we called it.

In a team meeting at the beginning of a series, we would "talk over" the other team. The manager would say, "How are they going to pitch to you?" I would say to myself that they're going to curve, so I looked for curves the whole day, the whole game, every time I came to bat. Remember, that now I'm talking about the average pitcher.

The other club would be in *their* meeting, talking us over. I'll bet they said, "Any time you got men on, give Berger the curve ball." The curve ball you're likely to hit on the ground. So for years I looked for the curve ball. They didn't change. They didn't cross you up, except for a hard-throwing guy.

With speed ball pitchers who threw hard, I would never look for the curve. You had to protect yourself by looking for speed; you can get killed looking for a curve. In hitting the curve ball, you lay back for the break. If you do that and the pitcher throws a fast ball at you, you can't get out of the way.

You don't step into a curve; you just wait for it. You let yourself sit at the plate. You could step across, or toward the ball, but if you do that they'll pitch on your hands. Hornsby hit that way, but he was in a class by himself. He stood way back in the box and stepped toward the plate. If the pitchers threw outside, he'd hit them down the right-field line, and to right center.

There's a lot of skill to hitting and in most cases it's a gift of nature. The one big exeption that I recall was Joe Cronin. When I was in high school with him, he couldn't hit worth a damn. We used to work out in San Francisco at Balboa Park. We'd go up there and hit all day. He tried all the stances and finally came up with one that worked for him – because he had a lifetime average of .301 after twenty years, and he made it to the Hall of Fame.

The big guys have the power. They scare the pitcher when he knows that they can hit him one-handed over the fence, or drive a bad pitch out of the park. They're strong enough to pull that bat around. They can hit a ball that's four or five inches outside and pull it over the fence.

Six hundred feet, I believe, is about as far as anybody can hit them. I don't think that mechanically and physically you can hit them any farther. Most of the great distance hitters, by the way, were from six feet to six-feet-two inches tall and weighed between 180 and 210 pounds. Very few big, strong men can play baseball well.

In Oakland there was a player named Roy Carlyle who hit one over the center field clubhouse against a building across the street. It put a mark up there. It was hard to believe. It was a drive that must have been six hundred feet. Carlyle was six feet, two-and-a-half inches tall and weighed 195 pounds. He had played with Washington and Boston in the American League in 1925-26.

If you hit a ball good, it's going to go out. I never thought that 350 feet was a great drive, but anytime you hit them 380 feet and up, you were hitting them pretty good. I still think that 395 feet is a fairly good poke, but not to extra power hitters like Babe Ruth, Hank Greenberg, Frank Robinson, Johnny Mize and maybe a dozen others. That was no drive to them.

Today 395 feet often looks like no drive at all. I've seen those little skinny guys hit them that far. As I watch them, I think that either the ball is a jack rabbit or the hitters have muscles hidden someplace. Maybe when they moved home plate up or shortened the fences, they forgot to change the signs.

If we had a film of Babe Ruth hitting, you would see what I mean. He was six feet, two inches tall, and in his prime weighed about 215 pounds. He stood up there pigeon-toed with his right leg, foot and toes turned toward his left foot. He had his back to the pitcher! Then he'd bring that bat down to his side. He'd start from there and wind up and swing. When he let loose, you could see him unwind.

Everything went into it – his whole body – hips, shoulders, arms, wrist – everything went – all 215 pounds. Now, when you've got everything coordinated like that, you're going to get the distance; Ruth hit them 600 feet many times.

Of course, there were always exceptions. Hack Wilson was only 5'6", but he weighed 190 pounds and had a powerful build. Moreover, he was remarkably fast. Mel Ott was five-feet-nine and weighed only 170, and Willie Mays was five feet ten-and-a-half and also 170. Both men, however, were quite strong and had remarkable coordination. In addition, they were very durable.

They both started young and lasted twenty-two years. Frank Howard, on the other hand, stood six-feet-seven and weighed

181

255 pounds. In baseball, he was considered to be a giant. Surprisingly, he was pretty durable, too, surviving for sixteen years.

In comparing myself with other outfielders in the National League in my time, I'm not ashamed to put myself up there with any of them. I was a good outfielder, playing center field. I was an excellent base runner, having learned my lessons well with Marty Krug in Los Angeles. I was the fastest man on the Boston team. I didn't have an overpowering arm, but it was good enough.

I wouldn't compare myself with a hitter for average like Paul Waner, for example, but overall I think I was as good as anyone. My batting average for ten years in the National League was an even three hundred. I had power and I hit the ball very far. Playing for most of the time in home parks that were difficult for home runs, I averaged twenty-four a year and there wasn't any park in the league that I couldn't hit it over.

Braves Field in Boston was a big ball park, and it was also very windy, usually to the disadvantage of the hitter. Sluggers didn't like to go in there. Old-timers will tell you that it was a tough park. We called it a "pitcher's park," because a pitcher could make a mistake and not get hurt. He could pitch a fast ball high and the hitter would hit those long fly balls to deep center over 400 feet – but it would just be another out. In those days, 400 feet was a good drive. The ball was not too lively; in fact, it was a little dead.

My other home park for two years, Crosley Field in Cincinnati, was noted for few home runs. In one season, for instance, visiting teams hit only eighteen home runs, and the home team hit the same number, for a grand total of thirty-six.

As a slugger I rate myself with Mel Ott of the New York Giants and Chuck Klein of the Phillies. I was always neck and neck with them in home runs, but they drew away from me near the end of the year.

I have a good argument in making that comparison. I was a right-handed hitter playing in a tough park. They were left-handers playing in the two parks where the home run production was highest year after year, and where the right field line was very short.

There are always so many things to take into account, which the average fan doesn't realize. Take the season of 1931 in the National League, for example. The heavy thinkers decided that too many home runs were being hit, so they brought in a ball with a raised seam. It not only made the ball less lively, but it gave the

pitchers more stuff. The ball would break better and sink better.

Early in the season in Boston I learned what that meant. I hit a ball as hard as I ever hit one and it didn't go out of the park – in fact, it sunk. I knew that I wasn't going to hit many out of the park with that ball. I decided that I'd better go for the batting average, so I just tried to meet the ball. I tried to hit through the box straight away, or where the ball was pitched.

I wound up with 199 hits, but with only nineteen home runs – half of what I had hit the year before, but I raised my batting average to .323 and hit 44 doubles – second-highest in the league.

It was a good year, I thought, until I got a letter from Judge Fuchs. To my surprise he suggested that I take a 10% cut in salary, but I responded, "Hell, I had a great year." (Elsewhere I discuss the struggle over pay.) I discovered you can't win in the discussion with the owners. If you have a high batting average, they say, "Yeah, but you didn't hit as many home runs." If you go up in home runs, they say, "But your batting average dropped so many points." I didn't take that cut, but I didn't get much of a raise, either.

B. Baseball as a Career

Wally tells why he chose baseball as a career, how he persisted, and what it meant to him. If he had known what the odds were against his making it to the major leagues, he might not have dropped out of Mission High after his junior year.

C. A. Aldington, in *Baseball Magazine* for June, 1938, reported that "Last season (1937), 10,000 minor league contracts passed through the office of the National Association." Whenever a new player signed a contract, a card with his name was filed with the Association. In that year there were 85,000 cards in the files of the Minor League Association.

But Wally didn't know the odds, so he persevered. When he got a chance to play in the Miners' League at Butte, he left his job at the Nicolai Door Company. At that point, the company offered him an advancement to shipping clerk at a good salary. He turned it down, got his savings out of the bank, and took the train to Butte.

Joe Cronin, a teammate of Wally's on the 1922 Mission High School Championship team, also beat the odds. He made it to the majors several years ahead of Wally and was manager of the Boston Red Sox in the years when Wally was playing across town with the Braves.

From the age of fifteen, I thought seriously about baseball as a career. At first I thought of the adventure and romance. I dreamed of going to New York, Chicago, Boston and all those places. Here was a way to travel. When I first left home, I would have played just for my expenses – for my room and board. I soon realized that I had to live in the winter – had to put something aside.

Stories about how tough it was in the minors didn't deter me. I remember a catcher named Andy Vargas who was farmed out by the Seals to Macon, Georgia. He was a short, roly-poly catcher. I saw him the winter after the season was over, and he was a sack of bones. "Andy, what the Hell happened? You've lost a lot of weight."

He replied, "You play down in the South there and it's a hundred degrees in the shade. It's humid and you sweat all the time. If you didn't have a beer or two, you'd die. The mosquitoes are so big you need pliers to pull them out of you." But when he talked about the girls – Macon had a women's college – it sounded good to me, but he hated it.

It took me the next ten years to get to the big leagues. There weren't any scouts looking at high school players. I played winters and summers in semi-pro ball for five years and became pretty well-known. Finally, I played with the Bertillion Hatters, an elite team in the winter league in San Francisco. Several times during those years I was about to give up, but something would always happen to keep me going.

Playing baseball was the only job in my life that I liked. All the other jobs, before and after, were just to make a living. I was never trained for anything else. Years later I thought that I should have gone to school in the off-season and studied geology. It always interested me, but by then it was water over the dam. You see, we didn't have any guidance counselors in high school. No one ever discussed those things with you. When I made the decision to quit high school, the vice-principal was cold and sarcastic to me.

One of the many reasons that baseball attracted me was the chance to make good money in a job that was pleasant and exciting. My family was poor. I was broke many times when I was a young man. Often I didn't have money to buy lunch, go to a show or anything else. I even walked to work many times in order to save a nickel instead of riding the streetcar.

In the early days, ball players were considered hoodlums. They stayed at third-rate hotels, sat around bars drinking and fighting and dressed like rowdies. By the time I came along, professional ball players – especially in the major leagues – had prestige. You got a lot of attention. People looked up to you, wanted to be around you.

You stayed at the best hotels. You dressed well – you didn't go around in sport shirts. You always wore a white shirt, tie and coat. In fact, Mr. Wrigley, owner of the Chicago Cubs, would buy all his players a felt hat in the spring. In the summer he bought each of them a Panama. He said to his players, "There's no excuse for going without a hat. You've got to look the part of a major league player. We stay in good hotels and I want you to look well."

Actually, when we walked into their hotel, there would be a big banner up in the lobby saying, "The CHICAGO CUBS are staying here." It would advertise the hotel. People would come there to see the ball players. In the lobby or dining room they could spot a ball player right away even in his business suit. His face was tan, he looked a little weather-beaten and the top of his forehead was white where it had been protected from the sun by his cap.

And just as they do today, there were the autograph hunters stopping you whenever they recognized you. The kids would hang around outside the park. In Brooklyn they would wait at the subway for you. As you walked the six blocks to the park, they walked along with you, asking for autographs all the way. I still get letters from kids who collect baseball cards, wanting me to sign them and send them back.

As I've mentioned several times, there was the fun of travel. Even after ten years in the majors, I always liked going on the road. I enjoyed visiting towns over and over again. I would sightsee every chance I got – historic places, museums and art galleries. I got up early in the morning, had a good breakfast and looked around town.

When I played with Boston, I was glad to go on the road for another reason. Not that I didn't love Boston, but our park was a great big one – it was a "pitcher's park," and I was a hitter. I hit better on the road in the smaller parks!

More than anything else was the thrill of the game, especially hitting. If it wasn't for hitting, you wouldn't play. You get great satisfaction in connecting with that ball – hitting it a mile. I liked to see how far I could hit them, and I could hit them pretty far. That was the big thrill. I bore down on hitting, practiced hitting.

However, I didn't neglect the other parts of the game. I

practiced fielding, running and everything else because I wanted to be a complete ball player. You couldn't just be hitting and be a lousy infielder or outfielder.

Today, of course, the teams in the American League have the designated hitter who just bats for the pitcher. So far the National League has turned down this idea. However, there was an interesting historical note on the designated hitter: The National League at its winter meeting in 1928-29 first considered it. *President John A. Heydler suggested to the owners the advisability of having a player to be named before a game began, act as batter for the pitcher, throughout... The suggestion was received with approval by some managers and owners, but with hesitation by others. Any plan of that character necessarily would meet with a plea for further consideration."* (Quoted from "Editorial Comment" by John B. Foster in *Spalding's Guide* for 1929.)

Then there is the great satisfaction of winning. Especially when you're a tail-end team, and you walk into some team that's leading the league and you knock them out of first place. It's a big satisfaction. You say, "We did it – and we're just as good as you!" It's still that way today.

Another interesting part of the life of a big-league player, in addition to all the publicity and attention given to baseball stars, was that you got to meet all kinds of people on all levels – something which would have never happened otherwise. In Boston, for instance, I lived in a neighborhood with Harvard professors and felt at home there. I received invitations to the homes of business and professional leaders, and I was in demand to make appearances at public events and at community organizations. I even got to know important people in politics and show business.

One of the greatest satisfactions of all was being on a team that lived and traveled together. I enjoyed the companionship and social activities of the players. It was being with the fellows. Every day you were part of a group which was striving together. There was the horseplay, the kidding, and the endless discussions about our experiences. In other professions they call it "shop talk."

As I got older, it became more important, and when I left baseball I missed more than anything else those friendships and associations. The pace of life was different then. We traveled by train and spent lots of time together from spring training to the end of the season in October.

Even in the winter time, ball players got together often to

play golf and participate in other activities. It seems quite different today with rapid air travel and other changes in the way we live and work.

The harsh fact is that the career of a ball player – or, for that matter, any career in professional sports – is likely to be very short unless the player becomes a coach, manager or scout. When you get to 35, you know what the club owners are saying to themselves about you: "He's got only a couple more years left at the most. If we can make a deal for him now, we'd better do it." You know what they're thinking. You see it happen all the time with other players, and you have to plan what you're going to do when you're out of baseball.

During my first year in Boston, I was reminded of what happens sooner or later to all ball players, even the greatest. We were playing in Chicago, and the great George Sisler was on third base. A fly ball was hit to the outfield – not too deep; Chicago's not a big ball park – Sisler tagged up and Kiki Cuyler threw him out at home. When George came back to the dugout, he said, "I'm through. If I couldn't beat that throw, I know I've lost my speed. I've slowed down."

I never forgot that. It was the last year Sisler played. I never saw him in his prime, but he was one of the greatest players ever. He had over two hundred hits a season six times. In 1920 he made 257 hits and in 1922 he had 246. He batted an amazing .407 in 1920 and an incredible .420 in 1922.

What happens is that a player's legs give out first, but he can still hit. He can still see pretty good. He doesn't lose the power of hitting, but as he gets older his reflexes are a little bit slow, and he starts to get more selective. He's looking for one he can powder, but the pitchers up there have good control; he's not going to get that pitch. You have to learn to hit a ball that's a little bit bad—a few inches inside, a few inches outside. Of course, inside was my power. If they pitched me a low inside ball, I'd golf it out of the park.

Later in my career when I was with Cincinnati, I was hitting against one of the Giants' pitchers and I was taking balls a couple of inches outside. Harry Danning, the catcher, said, "You know, Wally, you used to hit those...you're not going to get them down the middle...what are you hitting?"

"Oh, around .250," I replied.

"See what I mean?" he said, "You used to hit those balls that were a little bit bad." I saw what he meant, all right. At first you don't think you've lost any of your speed. You're throwing all right, but you're not hitting as well as you did.

A sports writer says in the paper that you're half-a-step slower. They said it about me and I didn't like it because I didn't think I was. Then you think, "Maybe I'm getting thrown out when I used to beat them out." I was always very fast and I still thought I could run. I didn't like to hear that I was slowing up. Of course it finally happened to me, and like a lot of players today, I knew when I was about washed up.

So your career is over in baseball at an age when other professionals are just getting established. The majority of players in my time were working people. There were only a few college graduates. I don't remember anyone I played with who came from a wealthy family.

Many players had trades to fall back on. They were carpenters, plumbers or bartenders, and they'd work at their jobs on the off-season. Bill Urbanski, the Braves' shortstop, was a barber. A large number of players came from rural areas, and they thought of buying a ranch or a farm when their playing days were over. Since I didn't have the education or a trade, I thought I would go into some kind of business. I had saved my money, but in those depression times it was hard to know which way to go.

APPENDIX

1.

BOSTON NATIONAL LEAGUE BASE BALL COMPANY
BRAVES FIELD, BOSTON

January 13, 1930

Mr. Walter Berger
406 East 42nd St.
Los Angeles, Calif.

Dear Mr. Berger:
    Enclosed please find contract for $750 per month, which represents the usual increase over the salary received from your former club, with a hope that your work will warrant a far more substantial increase in your contract for 1931.
    Please sign contract and return at your earliest convenience, reporting to Manager McKechnie, at the West Coast Inn (opposite the ball park), St. Petersburg, Fla., on February 28th. Your transportation will be returned to you by Mr. Cunningham, our secretary, on your arrival.
    Wishing you a happy and successful new year, I am,

Sincerely yours,

(S) Emil E. Fuchs
President.

2.

BOSTON NATIONAL LEAGUE BASE BALL COMPANY
BRAVES FIELD, BOSTON

January 8, 1931

Mr. Walter Berger
456 1/2 E. 43rd St.
Los Angeles, Calif.

Dear Walter:
    Enclosed please find a contract for $7000, which is an increase of $3000 over last year's contract.

I went over the situation with Manager McKechnie and we both appreciate that you, for a first year man, made a very creditable showing. I am personally adding an extra $500, which I do not desire to have appear in the contract, but upon the signing of same by you we shall mail you a check for $500, which is my method of giving you an extra reward for your diligent, faithful service and as a medium of encouragement to you.

My methods with reference to salaries has always been to give the players who remain with us some increase each year, depending, of course, upon their ability, deportment, and value to the club. You can readily understand, therefore, that with an increase as substantial as the enclosed, if you can show the progress already indicated by you, you can anticipate a further increase each year as time goes on, which I hope will put you in a position of being one of the well paid ball players in the major leagues.

There is nothing further to add except that I believe you will appreciate our desire to be entirely fair with you, and therefore you will also understand that the enclosed contract, which we hope will be satisfactory to you, is a final one. My method has been and always will be to give what I think is fair, to avoid any future correspondence and disputes.

Judge Landis 'phoned about your playing ball during this last month on the coast, which, of course, is contrary to baseball law. I wired him that in my opinion you had misinterpreted and misunderstood the rule.

I hope that you will continue to have a pleasant winter and that we shall meet at St. Petersburg, where you will please report to Manager McKechnie at the West Coast Inn on the morning of Wednesday, February 25th.

With warm regards to Mrs. Berger, I am,

Sincerely yours,

(S) Emil E. Fuchs
President.

P. S. Please return signed contract immediately in order that Manager McKechnie may determine on whom he can count, as this year's rule prohibits any player from spring training camp whose contract is unsigned. You will be reimbursed by Secretary Cunningham upon your arrival for any money advanced by you for transportation expense.

3.

3125 Hollydale Dr.
Los Angeles, Calif.
Jan. 15, 1931

Dear Judge:

Contract and letter received and appreciate your attitude toward the increase of your players salary. It's only reasonable that a player expects an increase each year, but each case is different and I beleive that if you'll look into my case further you can readily see my reasons for feeling that the increase offered me is not sufficient.

Now, if we were taking last years salary as a basis it would be a very nice increase but I really dont feel that we should do that.

Last year if you'll remember I received practically no increase over my Coast League contract and accepted rather than argue so I could prove that I was of Major League ability.

I never have felt that I received my true worth last season so you can see why I don't feel that any increase with last seasons salary as a basis is fair to me.

In regards to the 500 dollar bonus offered to me I had felt that I was deserving of a bonus for last seasons work, so feel that your offer of that is for work done in the past and I assure you that the offer certainly is appreciated and lives up to your reputation for fairness.

I think that the amount tendered me for the coming year should be as to my true worth to the club and not an increase over last years contract.

I know the amount that I am asking of you sounds like a large jump but I feel that I drew enough fans through the gate and was popular enough with the Boston fans to be worth $10,000 a year to your club. Now Judge don't think me fatheaded but just look things over and if you were in my position. Would you take a cent less than $10,000 a year?

Hoping to hear favorably from you and best regards to everyone in the office. I am,

Sincerely Yours,

Walter Berger.

4.

BOSTON NATIONAL LEAGUE BASE BALL COMPANY
BRAVES FIELD, BOSTON

January 28, 1931

Mr. Walter Berger
3125 Hollydale Dr.,
Los Angeles, Calif.

Dear Walter:

Thank you for your nice letter of January 15th. Your argument is a very reasonable one in theory. In other words, if you had received a larger amount in accordance with your work, last year's contract would have been higher, and by the same process of fair increase, so would this year's contract have been larger, but let me tell you for your information, so that you are not misled, that no second year man in the history of baseball, that I know of or am able to learn of, ever received a $10,000 contract for his second year's services.

I believe that Manager McKechnie, who is intensely interested in your career and your future with him and the club, will tell you that. I have again talked with him and he is endeavoring to give you the benefit of every opportunity and advance possible. He feels that you have been fairly and justly treated, and so do I. My policy has always been to increase the salaries of my players as long as they are loyal, keep their heads, and so conduct themselves as to permit an increase.

You have a long way to go in baseball, and it is our hope that your last year's work will be improved upon in 1931, all of which will be appreciated and demonstrated by another increase, and more as the years go by. I honestly believe that if you were acquainted with the conditions that bring about large salaries, you would find that they come gradually and are based on justice to the player.

Your mention in your letter what I would do if I were in your position. Inasmuch as you make that statement I will answer it – if I were in your position, having in mind your youth and physical ability, I would sign the contract, say nothing more about it, remain the same modest young man that you have been, and demonstrate your right to the same consideration next year that you have received this. That is all that I can say or advise you on.

We must adopt a policy which we think is fair and stand by it; therefore I hope that you will follow the advice that you seek so that the relationship between you and the club can go on for years to come in the same pleasant manner.

Sincerely yours,
(S) Emil E. Fuchs
President.

5.

3125 Hollydale Dr.
Los Angeles, Calif.
Feb. 3, 1931.

Mr. Emil E. Fuchs,
Braves Field
Boston, Mass.

Dear Judge:

Your letter of the 28th received and am glad to know that you can at least see a part of my reasons for not signing the contract you have offered me.

I dont care to go into what other players have or do receive, their affairs have nothing to do with what I do. I can only bank my own check and that is what I'm interested in. As far as no other player receiving $10,000 a year in his second year, you know Judge, that there is always a first time for everything, and if I didn't feel that I was worth that amount, I wouldn't be asking for it.

I appreciate the interest that both you and Bill McKechnie have taken in my playing and also the advice you have given me regarding the contract, but Judge, I don't beleive you put yourself in my position when you wrote that.

If I signed that contract as you suggest, I would not be satisfied and I don't think that you would want anyone on your club that was not entirely satisfied with his contract.

I want you still to feel that I am the same modest fellow that I have always been but that I do feel that I am worth $10,000 a year to your club with that modesty. I sincerely hope that you will think over my case some more and can see your way to give me the increase that I think I should get.

This part of the game is strictly business proposition and while it may sound egotistical I think you will take it only as I mean it.

I think the Boston Club made money last year and I beleive that I helped make it and am entitled to the increase.

Sincerely yours,

Walter Berger.

6.

WESTERN UNION

BOSTON MASS

1931 FEB 12 AM 11 24

WALTER BERGER
3125 HOLLYDALE DR
LOS ANGELES CALIF

INASMUCH AS I WANT YOU THOROUGHLY SATISFIED I AM BREAKING A RULE IN GIVING YOU CONTRACT FOR SEVENTY FIVE HUNDRED AND ONE THOUSAND FOR SIGNING WILL BE COMPELLED TO DO WITHOUT YOUR SERVICES UNLESS YOU ACCEPT THESE TERMS

EMIL E FUCHS

7.

BOSTON NATIONAL LEAGUE BASE BALL COMPANY
BRAVES FIELD, BOSTON

Jan. 22, 1932

Mr. Walter Berger,
3125 Hollydale Drive,
Los Angeles, Calif.

Dear Walter:
Enclosed please find contract for 1932 calling for $10,000 for the season. In view of all conditions I am sure you will agree with us is reasonable in accordance with my promise in last year's correspondence.
With warm regards to you and Mrs. Berger, I am

Sincerely yours

(S) Emil E. Fuchs
President

Please report at the West Coast Inn, St. Petersburg Florida on March 1st. Pay transportation, including Pullman, and this will be refunded on arrival by Secretary Cunningham. Meal allowance while traveling will be at the rate of $4.00 per day.

8.

COPY.

St. Petersburg, Fla.
Feb. 19, 1932.

Mr. Emil E. Fuchs,
Braves Field,
Boston, Mass.

Dear Judge:

Received contract and letter and appreciate your attitude toward the increase in salary.

It is only within reason for a player to expect an increase with each successful year and the size of the increase in accordance to the value that he is to the club. In my case the amount tendered to me is not quite sufficient.

I came through with another succesful year, a better one in fact than the preceding one. I feel that I drew enough people at the gate and was popular enough with the Boston fans to be worth $12,000 a year to your club.

Now Judge, dont think I'm getting egotistical take this as a business proposition.

Hoping to hear favorably from you and with best regards to the gang at the office, I am

Sincerely Yours,

Walter Berger

9.

BOSTON NATIONAL LEAGUE BASE BALL COMPANY
BRAVES FIELD, BOSTON

St. Petersburg, Fla.
March 23rd 1932

Mr. Walter Berger,
St. Petersburg, Fla.

Dear Walter:

You are holding up a large number of contracts, which are all signed and completed, yours being the only one outstanding.

I hope and expect that our relationship will continue to be amicable and pleasant and my personal opinion is that you will do far better being guided by one, who always has had his players welfare in mind.

the player who holds out annually sometimes gets the shade the better of it but my experience is that in the end such demands are not forgotten and he generally loses by total.

Not only as a matter of comparison but for the reason as I explained to you that we expect you to be with the Braves a great many years, your salary both as a matter of duration and ability, will compare favorably with any one in the league, irrespective of club he may be on.

As we decided that the salary offered you for the coming season, every thing taken into consideration, is just and fair, it will not serve your best purpose to delay signing any longer.

Therefore, I must request that you sign same immediately and give same to Mr. Cunningham.

Very truly yours

(S) Emil E. Fuchs
President

10.

BOSTON NATIONAL LEAGUE BASE BALL COMPANY
BRAVES FIELD, BOSTON

January 11, 1933.

Mr. Walter Berger,
5915 So. Wilton Pl.
Los Angeles, Calif.

My Dear Walter:

We are endeavoring to demonstrate the falsity of the general impression that ball players are unconcerned as to what happens to the fortunes or misfortunes that befall an investor and stockholder of a ball club today.

We contend that the intelligent players know what is happening, not only in this country but throughout the civilized world, and therefore our Board of Directors, instead of placing an arbitrary figure of reduction, would like to point out to the baseball world that the members of the Braves team cooperated in a voluntary and reasonable cut to meet the depression conditions existing.

The example that was set in Baseball must appeal to every thoughtful unit, either making a livelihood from or interested in the national game. Judge Landis starts by voluntarily refusing to draw more than a nominal sum, so that the necessary functioning of his office may properly continue. President John A. Heydler voluntarily has reduced his own salary eighteen percent.

The president of your club has voluntarily reduced his salary twenty percent. Your manager, who has a written contract, has volunteered to reduce his salary upwards of ten percent.

The new players who are joining the Braves have already signified their desire to be recorded in favor of a reduction over their previous contracts elsewhere.

Every business enterprise in the country has either arbitrarily, or by general consent, reduced salaries from twenty to thirty percent. The minor leagues have reduced their salary limit over fifty percent. The various leagues, major and minor, have reduced their appropriation from twenty to forty percent. Every club of the major leagues has pledged itself to a largely reduced pay roll. In one of the outstanding clubs of this country, the players have voluntarily agreed to a substantial reduction, so that the Boston club, when all is said and done, will be found to have reduced less, and will not alter their custom of increasing the very low paid men so as to encourage them with a livable wage in spite of the depression.

I want you to have the following facts in mind when you answer this letter:

First - that we appreciate your efforts.

Second - that we have no complaint as to your playing ability and your showing.

Third - in 1931 and 1932 we had over half a million people attending our home games, but the stockholders have not yet been able to draw a dividend or a single dollar interest on their investment since their connection.

Fourth - If times and conditions are such in 1933 that the stockholders are able to draw 4 percent on the capital stock, whatever reduction you make in your contract this year will be given to you at the end of the 1933 season, and if times are better, the normal increase based on your work, will continue.

Fifth - In order for the stockholders to accomplish this modest end, the attendance at Braves Field for the year 1933 must total 650,000. this in ordinary times, should not be a hard task, if with our increased strength we can remain in the first division. In that event you are to keep this letter as evidence of our promise to refund to you any reduction from your 1932 contract.

I am confident your action will be such as to enable our club to point with pride to your cooperation and understanding.

Please answer this at once.

Sincerely yours,

(S) Emil E. Fuchs
President.

11.

BOSTON NATIONAL LEAGUE BASE BALL COMPANY
BRAVES FIELD, BOSTON

January 31, 1933.

Mr. Walter Berger,
5915 So. Wilton Pl.
Los Angeles, Calif.

Dear Walter:

I wrote you a letter, which I take it you have not yet received, owing perhaps to your not having been at home, but I believe if you had received it, you would have voluntarily suggested a contract such as the enclosed, i.e., $9000 for the season of 1933.

As February is here, I cannot wait longer for your voluntary suggestion, and, therefore, tender you a contract which was decided at a meeting of the Board of Directors as being fair, equitable and final.

I wish you would read my letter so that you can again appreciate what is going on. A $9000 contract in these times, where you are sure of receiving that amount in cash, is equal to $15,000 in normal times, and I therefore will ask you to kindly sign and return it at your earliest convenience, reporting to Manager McKechnie at the West Coast Inn, St. Petersburg, on the morning of March 6th.

With all good wishes, I am,

Sincerely yours,

(S) Emil E. Fuchs
President.

P. S. Kindly pay your own transportation; it will be refunded to you by Secretary Cunningham on your arrival at St. Petersburg.

12.

Culver City, California,
February 10, 1933.

Mr. Emil E. Fuchs, President
Boston Braves,
Braves Field,
Boston, Massachusetts.

Dear Judge:

Contract received. After due consideration I find the terms unsatisfactory and do not intend to take a cut in salary for the coming season.

I had a good season last year and expected a raise. In our talks last spring about contracts you impressed on me that I was going to be with your club for years, and after each successful year I was to get an increase in salary. You also told me that your policy was not to give large increases, but a fair one, and in time I would be better off, etc. I suppose you have forgotten all about that. I have not!

Inasmuch that I expected an increase, Judge, I will sign for the same salary as last year, and consider that I have received a cut in salary. This depression has not cut my expenses very much, and I will not go into lengthy detail to explain why at this time.

Don't believe that I am being unreasonable in asking for the same money that I received last year, and please consider this as my final proposition.

Hoping to have a favorable reply, I am,

Very truly yours,

Walter Berger.

P. S. My present address is 4049 Madison Avenue, C/O Morse Apartment, Apt. #203., Culver City, Calif.

13.

POSTAL TELEGRAPH

FEB 24 1933

WALTER A BERGER=
APT 203 4049 MADISON AVE CULVERCITY CALIF=

WE WIRED YOU TO REPORT ON TIME AND WE WOULD TREAT YOU FAIRLY AND THEREFORE EXPECT YOU TO REPORT ACCORDINGLY=

EMIL E FUCHS.

POSTAL TELEGRAPH

MAR 3 1933

WALTER A BERGER=
APT 203 4049 MADISON AVE CULVERCITY CALIF=

LETTER RECEIVED AND FIRMLY BELIEVE YOU SHOULD ACCEPT TERMS MY ADVICE IS YOU WIRE ME THAT YOU WILL REPORT ON TIME AND LEAVE MATTER OF DIFFERENCE TO MAN-AGER MCKECHNIE AFTER CONSULTATION WITH HIM AND MY-SELF AT CAMP IF I CAN GET TO STPETERSBURG DURING TRAIN-ING PLEASE WIRE ACCEPTANCE OF THESE CONDITIONS AT ONCE=

EMIL E FUCHS.

14.

BOSTON NATIONAL LEAGUE BASE BALL COMPANY
BRAVES FIELD, BOSTON

August 25, 1933.

Mr. Walter Berger,
c/o Boston Braves,
Boston.

My dear Walter:

Owing to the bad start we had this year, we would have to draw between now and the 3rd of September upwards of 160,000 people to come near the attendance of the previous years, in accordance with the promise made by Mr. Adams to the gentlemen of the club who received a cut in their 1933 salary.

I believe your spirit and the spirit of the club has done so much for Boston and the Braves that irrespective of whether or not that total is reached, I feel it is justly due you for me to re-instate the amount of your 1932 contract, and you will receive the proportionate share of the amount of your cut in your salary check on the various pay days left this year. The first check to have the added share will be your salary check of September 1st.

Thanking you for your devotion both to me personally and to Mr. McKechnie, as well as to the club, and knowing that this action will furthur (sic) install in you the desire to keep up the fight, I am, with warmest regards,

Sincerely yours,

(S) Emil E. Fuchs,
President.

15.

BOSTON NATIONAL LEAGUE BASE BALL COMPANY
BRAVES FIELD, BOSTON

January 17, 1934.

Mr. Walter Berger,
253 N. E. 14th St.,
Miami, Fla.

Dear Walter:

I enclose contract for $11,500.

I am endeavoring to be fair with each individual player and recognize your improvement last year. As soon as business conditions change, I hope to continue to improve the status of the men who are giving us the benefit of their ability, loyalty, skill and hustle.

Please sign and return the contract, for I hope you feel that my action entitles me to no further controversy, and if anything, your approval.

Sincerely yours,

(S) Emil E. Fuchs,
President

Suite 229, Hotel Touraine,
Boston.

16.

Copley Plaza Hotel,
Suite 19.

January 28, 1935.

Mr. Walter Berger,
3928 Sixth Ave.,
Los Angeles, Calif.

Dear Walter:

In spite of the large losses of the club last year, the bill which you mailed will be paid, as we are re-financing the club, and there will be no future danger of holding up even small bills.

Enclosed you will find a contract for $12,000 and there will absolutely be no use in arguing about it. the club is endeavoring to pay as much as any other club, but in the event that it may be, in your opinion, less than what you would obtain elsewhere, remember this - in the expenditure of hundreds of thousands of dollars, we are entitled to have a few ball players who can make good without insisting that they obtain contracts which cannot be met with the limited attendance.

If 1935 turns out right, and your record is good, you will have a good argument in 1936, but I will ask you to immediately sign this contract and return it, so that I may be able to say to the public that our players have met the spirit of our efforts to continue baseball here on a high plane.

With warm regards to Mrs. Berger and yourself, I am,

Sincerely yours,

(S) Emil E. Fuchs,
President.

P. S. Kindly report for training at the West Coast Inn, St. Petersburg, on Thursday, February 28th.

17.

February 7, 1935.

Mr. Walter Berger,
3928 Sixth Ave.,
Los Angeles, Calif.

Dear Walter:

I received your very kind letter, together with your contract, and I assure you, as time goes on, you will not regret your consideration and the kind message received today.

With warmest regards and best wishes to you both, I am,

Sincerely yours,

(S) Emil E. Fuchs,
President.

February 11, 1935.

Mr. Walter Berger,
3928 Sixth Ave.,
Los Angeles, Calif.

My dear Walter:

I do not have the exact amount of the outlay agreed upon between us, but I know it was something around this figure, and if you have not already received it, I shall ask you to let me know the exact amount. If it is overpaid you can return it to the club; if underpaid, we will pay you the balance.

Sincerely yours,

(S) Emil E. Fuchs,
President.

18.

BOSTON NATIONAL LEAGUE BASE BALL COMPANY
BRAVES FIELD, BOSTON

January 24, 1936.

Mr. Walter Berger,
3928 Sixth Ave.,
Los Angeles, Calif.

Dear Sir:

Enclosed find contract.

Please sign and return at your earliest convenience. We will then notify you when and where to report and transportation will be furnished several days in advance of your time to leave for the training camp.

Very truly yours,

(S) Bob Quinn,
President

19.

Los Angeles, Calif.
Jan. 31, 1936.

Mr. Bob. Quinn,
Copley-Plaza Hotel,
Boston, Mass.

Dear Sir:

Enclosed find unsigned contract.

I find the terms therein highly unsatisfactory and really had expected a substantial increase over my last year contract.

After playing on a losing team as last seasons Braves and with the teams spirit at a low level all year, I managed however, to keep on hustling and gave my best efforts at all times and achieved the distinction of leading the Nat'l League in two important departments in batting. These facts or records seem to me to have been overlooked entirely when this seasons contract was made out.

Therefore I am returning it unsigned and want one calling for $17,000 per season.

Hoping to hear favorably from you. I am,

Sincerely yours,

Walter Berger.

20.

NATIONAL LEAGUE BASEBALL CLUB OF BOSTON, INC.
NATIONAL LEAGUE BASEBALL FIELD
COMMONWEALTH AVENUE
BOSTON

February 7, 1936.

Mr. Walter Berger,
3928 Sixth Ave.,
Los Angeles, Calif.

Dear Sir:

I am rather surprised at your letter, While, of course, I do not blame you or any one else, to get as much salary as they possibly can, yet there are times when we get to the top salary where it is impossible to increase it. In other words, when we are getting the top salary we then have to hustle to stay there and continue to draw this salary.

I put a slight increase in your contract because I wanted you to feel that the present owners want to be fair to every one. I am sorry if you are dissatisfied, but we will not increase this contract this season, and I wish to state further that we do not want any player to report to our club who is dissatisfied.

We are trying to build up an entirely new ball club and hope to be able to do so, and if we find we have any players who do not want to play for us we will be glad to dispose of their services.

I am in a position to know the salaries paid in both leagues, and when I tell you frankly that you are one of the high salaried men in the National League, I am telling you the truth. Outside of possibly one catcher, and three or four pitchers, you are the best paid man in the National League, believe it or not. There are a couple of outfielders in the National League, whom I hesitate to name, because I do not want to make them feel badly – but neither of these men are getting within $2500 of what you have been offered, and if your report and you want me to prove it, I can do so. I do not believe you have given this any thought. Neither do I believe you have the slightest idea of the salaries being paid.

Now, as to your leading the League, hitting in runs – please take this in as kindly a way as I want to put it to your – I know you hit in 130 runs, and if you go through the files of the Sporting News (if you keep a file), you will find that a lot of runs that you hit in did not mean a thing. I do not say this now to hurt your feelings. I am only telling you the gospel truth. You know the club won only 38 ball games, and any man hitting in 130 runs should win more games than that himself.

No, sit down and think this over, analyze it carefully, and I am sure that you will see just what I am telling you is true. I am returning your contract and asking you to give it the consideration it deserves, but please do not sign it if you are not satisfied, because we have fully made up our minds that no dissatisfied ball players will be permitted to come into our camp and no ball player will be allowed to go on the hotel register, or receive transportation, nor will he be allowed to put on a uniform, who has not signed a contract.

Very truly yours,

(S) Bob Quinn,
President.

Note: Bob Quinn's statement in the fourth paragraph is not correct: "...Outside of possibly one catcher, and three or four pitchers, you are the best paid man in the National League, believe it or not."

Players' salaries were trade secrets in those days, but sportswriter Al Abrams found some old files of the Pittsburgh Pirates which listed Pie Traynor's salary in 1933 at $13,000; Paul Waner's at $15,000; and brother Lloyd Waner's at $12,500.

In my judgement, all three of these great players were underpaid, but they obviously made more than Wally, and none of them was a pitcher or catcher. (Paul Gregory, *The Baseball Player – An Economic Study*, Public Affairs Press, 1959.)

21.

Los Angeles, Calif.
Feb. 13, 1936.

Mr. Bob. Quinn,
Copley Plaza Hotel,
Boston, Mass.

Dear Sir:

I have given your letter lots of thought and am sorry to say that it has not made me feel any different towards signing the present contract.

I want you to understand that I appreciate the small increase and do not want you to think that I am hoggish or over estimate my worth or value, but I have judged myself in comparison with other players in the National League taking into consideration differences of teams, playing fields ect.

I not only hustled to win and I beleive that I am a team ball player but also hustled to keep my salary up and to increase it until the time comes that I am unable to produce.

As far as my record of runs batted in, I fully understand that <u>one</u> man can not win pennants. I know that it takes a group of men playing together, hustling, and as a group having good seasons, to have a winner.

If you bring up statistics, records ect, of ball players, such as you made light of mine, then discount the records of all ball players, they are as worthless as mine is to you. We could argue pro and con indefinitely about statistics, there is no use going into it that deep to find the true value of players.

What I do know of records is, that players have been cut in salary and even sent to minor leagues on account of these records. It is apparent that their value was based along these lines.

Maybe those runs that I batted in last year did not win all the games that they should have, but you can overlook the fact that in driving in these runs it kept the Braves in many a game, and even though the games were eventually lost, it was through no fault of mine.

You are right Mr. Quinn, I do not know exactly what other players receive and only have a faint idea. What I do know is only through hearsay the newspapers and to guess.

Furthermore I do not care what other players receive, it is their business and outlook. I am only interested in my own affairs.

So I am sending back the contract unsigned. I am disatisfied and did not intend to report for spring training until I was.

Sincerely yours,

Walter Berger.

22.

NATIONAL LEAGUE BASEBALL CLUB OF BOSTON, INC.
NATIONAL LEAGUE BASEBALL FIELD
COMMONWEALTH AVENUE
BOSTON

February 18, 1936.

Mr. Walter Berger,
3928 Sixth Ave.,
Los Angeles, Calif.

Dear Sir:

I am indeed sorry that you feel as you do, because as I told you in my former letter, men of the calibre of Medwick, whom I do not believe you will think is a bad ball player, did not get within $2500 of what you are offered. I can name several others, but as you say, there is no use in going into a long controversy and I do not intend to do so. I honestly believe that you are well paid and I believe that if you give it any thought you will think the same.

I do not want to get smart or fresh with you, but we just cannot increase this contract for 1936. If you do not intend to sign it, will you please wire me, collect, upon receipt of this, so that I will know just how to figure.

Very truly yours,

(S) Bob Quinn,
President.

23.

NATIONAL LEAGUE BASE BALL CLUB OF BOSTON, INC.
NATIONAL LEAGUE BASEBALL FIELD
COMMONWEALTH AVENUE
BOSTON

January 27, 1937.

Mr. Walter Berger,
3928 Sixth Ave.,
Los Angeles, Calif.

Dear Walter:

Enclosed find contract for 1937. Please sign and return to us at your very earliest convenience.

Our pitchers and catchers will report to the Pheil Hotel in St. Petersburg on the morning of February 25th.

Our outfielders and infielders will report at the same hotel on the morning of March 7th.

Upon receipt of your signed contract we will furnish transportation from your home to the training camp.

Very truly yours,

(S) Bob Quinn,
President.

P. S.   In order that you will be sure to have a room at St. Pete be sure and wire a day or two before you are to reach there. If the hotels are all filled wire Duffy Lewis Pheil Hotel St. Pete.

Bob

24.

GIANTS
OPERATED BY NATIONAL EXHIBITION COMPANY
POLO GROUNDS
NEW YORK

December 29, 1937

Mr. Walter Berger,
3928 Sixth Avenue,
Los Angeles, Calif.

Dear Wally:

Enclosed please find two copies of your contract for 1938, one of which is to be signed and returned to our Office at 104 West 42nd Street, New York City.

Please do not give out the signing of your contract to the Press, as we wish to announce it from our New York Office at the proper time.

You will be notified later as to the time and place to report for spring training.

Very truly yours,

(S) William H. Terry,
General-Manager

25.

Los Angeles, Calif.
Jan 6, 1938.

Bill Terry,
Polo Grounds,
New york, N. Y.

Dear Bill:

In returning contract unsigned I was surprise at the size of the cut. I really did not expect to be cut that much and hoped to receive the same salary as of last season.

I've never received any $2500.00 raises, that is outside of my first year in the Nat'l League and then I was only getting a small salary.

Bill, I know I'm capable of playing ball every day and know I can do a good job, and I don't feel that I've slowed up that much. I was handicapped at the start of the season with an injury and had a hard time getting started. Down deep in my heart I really beleive that I would have had a great season if I hadn't had that misfortune, prior to the accident, I was going better than I ever had at any other spring.

This is no alibi, just the way I feel and beleive in.

Well, that's about all I can say in my behalf. Hoping to hear favorably from you, I am.

Yours Sincerely,

Walter Berger.

P. S.   Had my finger examined by a doctor friend of mine. Said it would be O. K. It hadn't bothered me all winter.

26.

GIANTS
OPERATED BY NATIONAL EXHIBITION COMPANY
POLO GROUNDS
NEW YORK

January 24, 1938.

Mr. Walter Berger
3928 Sixth Ave.
Los Angeles, California.

Dear Mr. Berger:

We believe it will be of great benefit to you as well as to the club to have on file a doctor's full report of your physical condition so that in the event of sickness or injury there will be a complete report of your case.

We have arranged through Dr. George Winthrop Fish of New York City to have

Dr. Ezra Fish
Pacific Mutual Building
523 West 6th Street
Los Angeles, California

make a physical examination of you for your benefit and for the benefit of the club.

Will you, therefore, kindly arrange an appointment with Dr. Fish. The Club, of course, will bear all expenses both as to transportation and doctor's fees.

Cordially yours,

(S) Horace C. Stoneham,
President.

27.

GIANTS
OPERATED BY NATIONAL EXHIBITION COMPANY
POLO GROUNDS
NEW YORK

February 1, 1938

Mr. Walter A. Berger,
3928 Sixth Avenue,
Los Angeles, Calif.

Dear Wally:

Referring to your letter of the Sixth of January, in which you advise that you did not expect your salary to be reduced Twenty-Five Hundred Dollars ($2,500), I am sure that you agree with me that the amount both the Boston and New York Clubs paid you for services was very much out of line. Of Course, I appreciate that you were handicapped by a bad finger. At the same time, you must agree that your throwing has been badly handicapped by a sore arm. Whether or not your arm will improve enough to play regularly is something we will have to find out this spring.

The salary of Ten Thousand Dollars ($10,000) offered to you in your contract is what we think that you are entitled to for the 1938 season. We hope that your playing this year will warrant an increase next year that will offset the cut we will have to ask you to take now.

We are enclosing your contract with the request that you sign one copy and return it to this office as soon as possible.

Very truly yours,

(S) William H. Terry,
General-Manager

28.

GIANTS
OPERATED BY NATIONAL EXHIBITION COMPANY
POLO GROUNDS
NEW YORK

Mr. Walter Berger,
c/o Cincinnati Base Ball Club,
Cincinnati, Ohio.

Dear Sir:

Enclosed please find official release notice, advising you of the outright assignment of your contract to the Cincinnati Base Ball Club.

Very truly yours,

(S) Horace C. Stoneham
President

29.

THE CINCINNATI BASEBALL CLUB CO.
NATIONAL LEAGUE
CINCINNATI

November 22, 1938

Mr. Walter Berger
3928 Sixth Avenue
Los Angeles, Calif.

Dear Wally:

Herewith a 1939 contract, specifying a salary of $10,000.00 for the season, which is the same salary offered you by the Giants last season.

While you are probably not the great ball player you were when this high salary was established, yet I believe your work for our Club last year, particularly your general attitude and hustle, justifies our continuing on the same basis.

I want you to know that while Bill and I were both

disappointed that you did not hold up the splendid batting performance you gave most of the season, we were well satisfied with your work.

You will agree that it is a little unusual for a club like Cincinnati to pay a salary of $10,000 to an outfielder whose hitting record is not considerably in excess of .300, yet I want you to know that clubs do appreciate general hustle and attitude on the club. As I said before, your work, while not outstanding, was satisfactory and your general disposition, conduct, hustle, team play, etc. were fine and it is really that part of your performance that we are recognizing in continuing the salary at this high rate.

Please sign the original copy of the contract enclosed and return it at an early date.

With kind personal regards and best wishes for a pleasant winter, believe me

Very truly yours,

(S) Warren C. Giles
Vice-Pres. & Gen'l. Mgr.

30.

November 28, 1938.

Mr. Warren C. Giles
Cincinnati B. B. club
Cincinnati, Ohio.

Dear Warren:

Inclosed find my signed contract for the 1939 season.

The terms were very satisfacory and I appreciate the fact that you and Bill were satisfied with my work of last season.

I'm looking forward to having a good season this coming year and am anxious to get started. The weather out here has been very good and am taking advantage of it by playing plenty of golf practically every day.

With best regards to everyone, I am
Sincerely yours,

Walter Berger.

31.

THE CINCINNATI BASEBALL CLUB CO.
NATIONAL LEAGUE
CINCINNATI
December 27, 1939

Mr. Walter Berger
3928 Sixth Avenue
Los Angeles, Calif.

Dear Wally:

I was going to talk with you about your contract when you were here, but we were in the midst of making two or three deals in which you and two or three other players were involved. We were not able to work them out.

Inasmuch as I am sending out contracts to all of the players on our Club, I wanted to send you a contract. I want to be frank with you, however, and to say that I am not sure at this time that we plan to retain you on our Club. I mention this merely to tell you all the facts. I do want to say, however, that if we do decide to assign your contract somewhere, it will be only because we feel we can have a better balanced outfield setup; that is considering right-hand hitters, left-hand hitters, etc., and not because of any desire to assign your contract other than that.

You will agree of course that you had a very ordinary year hitting, which made your second successive year under .300 and as such you cannot expect to receive anything like the contract you have had the last three or four years.

I dislike very much making any drastic reduction in salaries. However, I believe, all things considered, a salary of $5500.00 would be a fair one.

You are a ten year man and have served every club you have played for conscientiously and well. However, I believe you realize that your performance on the field is getting to a point where you cannot expect more than the salary I am offering.

If you should be with our club all year and have an exceptionally good year, in our opinion, I will not hesitate to do something more for you at the end of the season, but all things considered, I believe the enclosed contract at $5500.00 is a fair one. Please do not misunderstand me, I think you are one of the greatest fellows I have had on a club, and I only wish that you had had a good enough year this past one so we would feel justified in continuing your salary at the rate you were paid last year.

If the enclosed contract is satisfactory, please sign and return it at your early convenience.

With kind personal regards, believe me
Cordially yours,

(S)Warren C. Giles
Vice-Pres. & Gen'l. Mgr.

32.

January __, 1940

Mr. Warren C. Giles
Cincinnati B.B. Club
Cincinnati, Ohio.

Dear Warren:

Received your letter and the contract. I am returning the contract unsigned. I anticipated a cut in salary but didn't dream that it would be such a drastic reduction.

You stated in your letter that "Inasmuch as you were sending contracts to all the players on the ball club that you wanted to send me one also." I'd like to ask one question. Just why did you want to send me one? It wasn't imperative, was it? The letter also cotained the fact that it was very possible that you may not retain me on the Club. Thank you for your fair warning. It's apparent that you hadn't been succesful in making a deal for me, I would appreciate it very much if you would give me my unconditional release.

Baseball being my livelihood and I sincerely feel that I have a few good years in me, I'd like to know definitely just what is what.

You also stated that you hate to make such drastic cuts in salary and that for two successive years I failed to hit 300 for the Cincinnati Ball Club. In 1938 I hit 298 including my N.Y. average but I did hit 307 the time that I played for the "Reds." I didn't receive any raise for my work that year. I really understand fully that I had a rotten season but in my opinion it was my first really bad year and I'm not satisfied at all to take such a drastic cut.

Well, I've spoken my piece and guess there isn't anything further to say. Hoping to hear favorably from you soon.

Sincerely yours,

Walter Berger.

33.

THE CINCINNATI BASEBALL CLUB CO.
NATIONAL LEAGUE
CINCINNATI

January 10, 1940

Mr. Walter Berger
3928 Sixth Avenue
Los Angeles, Calif.

Dear Wally:

I was not surprised that you felt the reduction in salary which I offered a very drastic one. I only wish now that I had discussed the matter of your contract with you in person rather than try and cover it by correspondence.

In your letter you ask why I sent you a contract because it was not imperative. Of course, it was not imperative but I usually do not wait until the last minute to offer contracts. This is born out by the fact that more than half of the club is already signed and if you will recall you received a 1939 contract at approximately the same respective date as you received your 1940 contract.

If you had not been a good fellow on the club, it would be easier to handle the situation from my standpoint. Possibly I was a little too frank in my letter to you, but you know me well enough to know that I try and give all the facts.

It is true, we did discuss with some other clubs the possibility of deals and in that conversation we discussed the possibility of including your contract in two or three that were discussed. You were not the only one, however, and you have been in baseball long enough to know that deals are discussed and changes are made on various clubs. We had secured waivers on you and even after securing waivers, I wrote the Chicago Cubs, thinking possibly they might be interested and ask if they would be willing to pay something approximating the waiver price even though it may be a little less. They replied by saying they were directing their efforts towards securing younger players unless they could get some outstanding player. That is no reflection on you, however, and I do not want you to take it as such.

Very frankly, we would like to secure someone for left field who might contribute more consisten in more effective hitting. As a matter of fact, we have nine outfielders on our roster and it is Bill's opinion and my own opinion that of the nine we do not have three whom we can count on a regulars in a sustained championship drive.

Without any intent whatever to deceive you or to indicate that you will be retained on our club all year, let me explain the situation as it may not have occurred to you. There was no outfielder on our club last year whose contract called for a higher salary than yours. Of the nine outfielders on our present roster, eight of them will be in the $4,000 to $7,500 salary bracket. The more nearly your salary approaches the salary of the other players we will be considering for left field or as extra outfielders, the more consideration you will be given. I believe you understand that. For example: When it comes time to cut down and we have two or three players in whom we consider there is very little difference in ability, it is only reasonable to assume that we would want to keep the player with the reasonable salary. In other words, we would not want to pay $6,500 to a player when we felt we could get the same performance from someone at $4,500 or $5,000. True you are entitled to some consideration because of your service and it was that thing that I gave some consideration to.

If you are willing to sign a contract specifying a salary of $5,500, I am willing to include in the contract a clause providing for a bonus of $1,500 if you are retained on the active list of the Cincinnati Club or any other Major League Club during the 1940 season. Inasmuch as you are a ten year man, this clause would in effect mean you would receive $7,000 as salary for 1940 or would sometime prior to the close of the 1940 season receive your unconditional release, and I consider this a very fair offer.

Most executives in my position give consideration to a player's general all around conduct, as well as his playing ability, although many of them do not. However, in your case, I want to say to you in all frankness that it is your general attitude, your hustle, etc. that prompts me to make this additional inducement to you. I trust you will see my position in this matter and find this latest offer acceptable.

Very truly yours,

(S) Warren C. Giles
Vice-Pres. & Gen'l. Mgr.

34.

THE CINCINNATI BASEBALL CLUB CO.
NATIONAL LEAGUE
CINCINNATI

January 22, 1940

Mr. Walter Berger
3928 Sixth Avenue
Los Angeles, Calif.

Dear Wally:

This acknowledges your recent letter, again returning your contract unsigned.

Apparently there is nothing more either of us can say at the present time because we have entirely different views respecting the matter of your salary for this year. It is possible that circumstances may change between now and the opening of the season which may cause either of us, or both of us, to view the matter differently.

I do want to comment, however, on your statement that you were part of the team that won its first pennant in twenty years and had the best year financially in this history, and that you thought everyone would share in its success. You did help us win, as did many of the others. I recognize that records do not mean everything. However, if one will consult the records I believe it is an easy matter to find that some player contributed to our success more than others. One of the main difficulties I have in trying to understand a player's viewpoint in salary negotiations is that when a player has a good year in performance on the field, he expects a very substantial increase. However, when his record is not so outstanding, some do not want to accept any reduction, and very few, if any, are unwilling to accept the same proportionate reduction that they expect when conditions are reversed.

It is true we did have a good year financially. I consider that you did also. You and other players were paid well and in addition received something more than $4,000 because of the success on the field. Players always seem to want to share in the financial success of the Club, but if the Club has a bad year financially they are not asked to contribute to the losses.

I, too, wish I had had a chance to discuss this matter with you, or rather had taken the opportunity to discuss it when you were in Cincinnati, as I am confident we would understand each other's views a great deal better. I do not want you to believe that I am arbitrary in this matter, as I really want to be fair, but I cannot quite bring myself to the point of justifying anything more than I have offered at this time.

Very truly yours,

(S) Warren C. Giles
Vice-Pres. & Gen'l. Mgr.

35.

January 26th 1940

Mr. Warren C. Giles
Cincinnati Baseball Club Co.
Cincinnati, Ohio.

Dear Warren:

Acknowledging your letter of January 22nd. I take this to be in the form of an ultimatum, but before we break off in corresponding, I'd like to bring up a point or two in regards to a players viewpoint concerning salaries.

I suppose it is reasonable to expect ball players to ask for a substantial increase in salary after they have a good season on the field but they also should expect a proportionate reduction after a mediocre season. At any rate I've felt that way about it, but it doesn't always work out that way.

I received a nice increase in salary in 1930 after the great season that I had that year, but outside of that I've never received substantial raises for the following seasons in which I did good work.

Going back to the season of 1935, I was fortunate enough to lead the Nat'l League in homeruns and runs-batted-in, I hustled all that year even though the team finished a very poor last; I was rewarded for my efforts to the tune of an $500 raise. After a little wrangling, I accepted, but with the thought in mind that I would be treated fairly in the event I was to have a poor year.

I recall another year, I took a $1000 cut because the Club argued the fact that it had lost money and also that conditions throughout the country were very bad and was in the throes of a depression, well I signed that contract even though I batted 307 or thereabouts. I was entitled to a raise that season and at the worst should have received the same contract.

I firmly believe that I've always been fair when it came time to discuss terms and usually signed my contract at the Clubs conditions.

Yes, I agree with you, if anyone would consult the records they will find that some players contributed more to the success of the club than other, but, those players were rewarded for their fine work in the field and at the plate. I'm sure these players received contracts that were highly satisfactory.

What I wanted to bring out is, that if am to be cut I'd like to be cut proportionately, the same way that I received increases.

Yes, I had a good year financially last year and the World Series money helped make it so, it was appreciated and would like to participate in another one, but a player can't depend on getting that extra money every year. At least I've never depended on it.

Well Warren, I guess that is about all that I have to say, there is no ill feeling on my part and I'm sure none on yours, we just can't get together on this business matter. I sincerely hope something will come up between now and the opening of the season that will be favorable to both of us.

Sincerely yours,

36.

THE CINCINNATI BASEBALL CLUB CO.
NATIONAL LEAGUE
CINCINNATI

February 17, 1940

Mr. Walter Berger
3928 Sixth Avenue
Los Angeles, Calif.

Dear Wally:

I have delayed answering your letter of January 26th because of being away a great part of the time and being terribly busy while here with the construction of new offices, etc.

I note in your letter of January 26th that you take my letter of January 22nd in the form of an ultimatum. I am very sorry if the letter sounded that way. I have never made it a practice of delivering ultimatums to any player, as I believe the question of salary is always a matter of negotiation and as I have said before, there are two sides to it - the player's side and the club's side, - and I have never yet resented a player expressing all his views and I do not want players to take offense at my expressing my views.

I do not know what your experience has been in the

past respecting increases and decreases. However, I believe you will agree that the salary rate you were paid last year was established at a time when you were having successively good years.

One of the biggest differences of opinion I find between players and myself in adjusting salaries is that where there is a change in the salary rate, either an increase or a decrease, the player is inclined to look at the amount of increase or the amount of decrease rather than at the actual salary that will be paid him. In other words, many of them look at the hole in the doughnut rather than at the doughnut. If we would just forget what you were paid or what the amount of the increase or decrease is and look at the amount of salary, you will receive in 1940, because after all that is the important thing, we could probably come to terms.

It is customary to establish salaries on the past year's performance and I have discovered in all my salary negotiations with players that if they have a good year they certainly do not hesitate to ask for the big increase. Some of them even want their salaries doubled. But when there comes along a bad year, they either want to maintain their past salary rate or take a reduction of $500 or $1,000.

As I said before, the important thing is what is the actual salary that will be paid irrespective of any comparison with past salaries.

The contract I offered you assured you of $7,000 or your unconditional release before the close of the season, and I was confident, of course, that you would receive the $7,000. If you have any objection to any part of the salary being conditional, I am willing to eliminate that phase of it. I am willing to offer you a flat salary of $7,250 in an effort to induce you to sign a contract immediately so as to be in our camp on time. You have been a very decent fellow and while we have a difference of opinion regarding your salary for the next year, you have been fair in your negotiations.

Frankly, I do not want any adverse publicity respecting your contract. Such things tend to effect the player adversely more than the Club, particularly if the player has not had an outstanding record. In other words, if publicity should be given to the fact that you and I are having difficulty over your contract, such publicity would be more harmful to your popularity than it might be to others who had an outstanding year.

I do not know exactly how to express this to you, but you are the kind of fellow who seems to go better when the fans are "in your corner," and I must say that some plays in the World Series games have had an effect of alienating the fans affections in the case of two or three ball players on the club, and one of them unfortunately is you.

In other words, if you are to be in our camp, I do not want you there with the public in general believing we do not have confidence in you, and the fact that you and I should be having any difference of opinion over salary might make people believe that we did not think as much of you as we really do.

For your information, I have arrived at the $7,250 figure by striking an average of the salaries of the outfielders already signed on our club. In fairness to you, I have included only four outfielders, Goodman, Craft, DiMaggio and Gamble. If I should have included McCormick, of Indianapolis, on whom we get very favorable reports and in whom we have quite an investment, and had also included Luce and Galatzer, the average salary would have been brought down considerably. However, the $7,250 salary I am offering you compares favorably with the average of the salaries the four other outfielders have already signed for. When I say 'compares favorably,' I mean it is within $80 of the average. I do not believe you could reasonably expect to be paid more than the average paid to the other four outfielders, when the average included Goodman, one of the outstanding outfielders in the League.

At any rate, I am enclosing a new contract specifying a salary of $7,250, with no conditions, which I trust you will find acceptable, and if it is acceptable, I would appreciate your wiring me immediately upon receipt of this letter, and returning the signed contract by letter. If you are not going to accept it, I also would appreciate your wiring me, upon receipt of this letter, because I want to know at the earliest possible date whether this offer is acceptable to you.

With kind regards, believe me

Very truly yours,

(S) Warren C. Giles
Vice-Pres. & Gen'l. Mgr.

37.

Feb 19, 1940

Mr. Warren C. Giles
Cincinnati Baseball Club Co
Cincinnati Ohio

Dear Warren:
    Enclosed find my signed contract, the terms were satisfactory.
    I intend to leave for Tampa as soon as I can get my house and business in order. I'm pretty sure that I will be able to leave by the end of this week. I'm motoring and barring any unforseen delays hope to be in Tampa by the 1st of March.
    I do not intend making any predictions for myself and all that I can say for now is that I'm going to give the "Reds" all that I've got and hope to plays lots ball in that "Leftfield."
    With kindest regards, I am.

Sincerely yours,

38.

THE CINCINNATI BASEBALL CLUB CO.
NATIONAL LEAGUE
CINCINNATI

May 11, 1940

Mr. Walter Berger
Rosedale Apartments
3637 Rosedale Place
Cincinnati, Ohio

Dear Wally:

    As I told you yesterday, it is not an easy job for one in my position to be obliged to give a player like yourself an unconditional release.

    While you have not been with our Club long, I feel, from conversations with Bill McKechnie and from my associations with you and from observing your actions, that I do know you well.

Your conduct, hustle, habits and general attitude toward the management and office have all that anyone could ask or expect. In fact, I have never had contact with a player who seemed more conscientious or who gave the management and office as little trouble and as little concern as you.

As explained to you yesterday, it was necessary to reduce our player roster to the limit of 25 men by midnight May 15. Naturally we wanted to keep those whom we felt would help us the most. The waiver thing also entered into it. Being unable to make a deal in the National League, it was necessary to reduce our roster by transferring or releasing those players on whom we could secure waivers. The only reason for releasing you was because of the necessity of reducing our roster and the belief that those whom we were keeping might be of more value to the Club on the field. We may have made a mistake and may be keeping players who will prove to be not of as much value as you.

I want you to know we do appreciate what you did for our Club when you first joined us. We also appreciate your splendid attitude, and I am hopeful that you are able to get on with some other Major League Club, as I truly believe you have sufficient ability to help any one of several Major League clubs. If there is any way I can assist you in getting lined up somewhere to your entire satisfaction, I will be only too glad to do so.

With kind regards, believe me

Very truly yours,

(S) Warren C. Giles
Vice-Pres. & Gen'l. Mgr.

39.

THE CINCINNATI BASEBALL CLUB CO.
NATIONAL LEAGUE
CINCINNATI

May 11, 1940

Mr. Walter Berger
c/o Philadelphia Baseball Club
Drake Hotel
Chicago, Illinois

Dear Wally:

This acknowledges yours of May 29th.

It did not occur to me until after receiving your letter that you were not paid the additional ten days salary to which you were entitled. As a matter of fact, when your letter was received, I remarked here in the office that I was sure you were paid that extra ten days pay. However, on checking it out with Bill Bramham, I found that the check was made out for your salary only through May 10th. Your certainly are entitled to the extra ten days pay. I may have been confused by having the transaction take place on the 10th of May. I thought when I asked Bill Bramham to make out your check that I asked him to make it out through the tenth, plus ten days' pay, and that is what I thought was delivered to you, as I didn't examine the check when it was handed to me.

I am glad you wrote me about it because if you had not, it would have completely escaped my attention.

I am enclosing herewith our check in the amount of $429.76, covering salary at the rate of your Cincinnati contract, May 11th, through May 20th.

I am glad you were able to get on with the Philadelphia Club and you have my very best wishes for a successful season.

Cordially yours,

(S) Warren C. Giles
Vice-Pres. & Gen'l. Mgr.

GEORGE MORRIS SNYDER *(left)*
Teacher, sociologist: high school, college, adult education.

Saw Lefty Grove pitch for World Champion Philadelphia
Athletics; heard Howard Ehmke describe his World Series
performance in 1929 against the Chicago Cubs; saw Connie
Mack wave his scorecard.

WALTER ANTON BERGER *(center)*
One of the greatest outfielders in baseball during the
"Depression Decade."

Mission High, city champs San Francisco, 1922; semi-pro in San
Francisco with Modern Woodmen, Bertillion Hatters, *et al.*,
1922-26; Butte Miners and Pocatello Bannocks, 1927; L. A.
Angels in the Pacific Coast League, 1928-29; Boston Braves,
1930-37; New York Giants, 1937-38; Cincinnati Reds, 1938-40.

JACK SPENCER McCLAIN *(right)*
Artist, teacher; Member, Screen Writers' Guild.

Received first BRAVO award, in 1982, by the Los Angeles
Music Center Educational Division for Superior Achievement in
Arts Education (fine arts, television production, film classes).

Sculptor, painter, muralist, writer, cinematographer.